# Gods and Myths of
# Ancient Egypt

# GODS AND MYTHS OF ANCIENT EGYPT

Robert A. Armour

With the research assistance of
Alison Baker

THE AMERICAN UNIVERSITY IN CAIRO PRESS

**For Elizabeth**

Dar el Kutub no. 4130/85
ISBN 977 424 113 4

Printed in Egypt by The American University in Cairo Press

# Acknowledgments

My deepest thanks go to

John Rodenbeck and Jill Kamil—may Thoth as divine author and publisher guide and inspire their endeavors;

my wonderful students at Al Azhar and Ain Shams Universities in Cairo—may they continue in the traditions established at the library of Ra at Heliopolis eons ago;

my numerous guides in museums, tombs, and temples in Egypt—may Horus, the ultimate guide of the underworld, honor them all;

Leandra Garrett Armour and Elizabeth Pope Armour for sharing these stories and offering advice on their retelling—may the Great Mothers Hathor, Isis and Mut nurture and love them;

Alison Baker for her insights and enthusiasm—may she and Hathor share love, beauty, and wisdom for ever;

my American colleagues Walter Coppedge, Elizabeth Reynolds and George Longest, for reading the manuscript and trying to keep my ideas and English clear—may Ptah as creator and artist bless their labors in behalf of colleagues and, most especially, students;

Connie Lilly, Win Harrison, and Randy Anderson in Academic Computing Virginia Commonwealth University, who taught me word processing—may Thoth bring them blessings for this most useful advancement in the mysteries and magic of writing;

the staff at the Fulbright Commission in Cairo who gave support and resources without which this book could never have been written—may Anubis, the watchdog of all those who serve others, protect them;

all my friends from Cairo, especially Norm Gary and the Kritskys, who were always on the lookout for some book I needed or had time to listen to just one more wonderful story I had to tell someone—may Osiris provide them all with beer and wine to comfort their days and nights;

the International Communications Agency, the Council for the International Exchange of Scholars, and the Fulbright Commission in Egypt for giving me a year to teach and learn in Egypt—may all the gods find funds for them to offer to others such experiences as I had.

## A Note on the Illustrations

The illustrations for this book were mostly taken from line drawings in Ridolfo V. Lanzone, *Dizionario di Mitologia Egizia* (Torino, Italy: Litografia Fratelli Doyen, 1881-1885). These have been supplemented by drawings from E.A. Wallis Budge, *The Nile: Notes for Travellers in Egypt* (London: Thos. Cook and Sons, 1892) and H.M. Tirad, *The Book of the Dead* (London: Society for Promoting Christian Knowledge, 1910). The photographer was Professor J. Maurice Duke, to whom go special thanks for a difficult and arduous task.

# Contents

Preface ........................................................... 9

Chapters

1. Mythological Stories .................................. 11
2. The Great Ennead of Heliopolis ................ 15
3. The Adventures of Ra ............................... 58
4. The Adventures of Osiris and Isis ............ 72
5. Horus ...................................................... 89
6. Horus' Battle with Seth ........................... 98
7. Hathor .................................................... 110
8. The Triad of Memphis ............................ 120
9. The Triad of Thebes ............................... 137
10. Thoth and Maat .................................... 152
11. Anubis .................................................. 168
12. Three Fertility Gods ............................. 178
13. Postscript ............................................. 188
Appendix: Checklist of Characters from Egyptian Mythology. 190
Selected Bibliography ................................. 199
Index ......................................................... 203

7

# Preface

Having spent two decades as professor of literature and cinema, I have developed a scholarly interest in mythology, but I am not a trained Egyptologist. During an extended stay in Egypt, I realized that there was no contemporary book that set out in clear narrative the stories of the gods of ancient Egypt. I discovered that fragments of the stories were scattered here and there in various texts—some religious, some archaeological—and I made it my special occupation and pleasure to collect the tales and retell them in modern English.

In this effort I have been greatly indebted to Egyptologists who have done so much important field work to uncover the various documents and monuments that preserved the fragmented stories, which then needed someone to come along and bring them together. Without the fine work of many dedicated scholars, this book could never have been written, and to them I give credit for whatever factual accuracy is in it.

In attempting to uncover the most interesting tales from the most reliable sources, I have relied on the work of the most distinguished and careful scholars. Many of the earlier ones, such as E.A. Wallis Budge, Flinders Petrie, and James Frazer, collected material that remains valuable for anyone compiling the stories of Egyptian mythology. Their interpretations of it have been modified by more recent scholarship, but their pioneer collections preserved important material for later scholars to work on. Generally I have tried to rely on more contemporary books for interpretation.

For any study of Egyptian mythology and religion, the most fundamental sources are the ancient texts written during the

Pharaonic period. Egypt did not have a Homer to tell the stories, but it does have some of the most ancient religious writings—however fragmented—which have supplied latter-day scholars with much material. The oldest are the Pyramid Texts, beginning about 2345 B.C. These texts were taken from hieroglyphic inscriptions on the walls of pyramids built for kings during the fifth and sixth dynasties. The ancient Egyptians believed that after death their kings would need knowledge of the underworld in order to achieve immortality, and they provided this information carved on the walls of pyramids, as in that of Unas at Sakkara. A few centuries later it was no longer feasible to build a pyramid for every king, and the texts were preserved in a less conspicuous manner. During the Middle Kingdom, messages for recently departed kings and high officials were carved on their coffins, giving us the Coffin Texts. Even this method was impractical, and priests resorted to having the texts copied onto papyrus scrolls which could be illustrated and placed inside a coffin or tomb. The collected information from these scrolls makes up the famous Book of the Dead and dates from the early New Kingdom (c. 1567-1320 B.C.). Despite its name, this is not a single book but a compilation of numerous texts; and even as gathered together by later scholars, the Book of the Dead does not present a systematic theology or mythology.

These various sources have preserved for us fragments of ancient Egyptian religion and mythology, but were it not for graphic portrayal in Greek and Roman writings, even such myths as those of Osiris and Isis would be largely unintelligible from the brief, partial references in Egyptian texts.

The hieroglyphics from pyramid and coffin walls and papyrus scrolls have been compiled and translated in English versions, which are referred to along with other sources in the bibliography. (Students should note that in this study I have modernized the language of these translations.)

Where possible, the spelling of Egyptian proper names and the dates for Egyptian history in this book follow those used in Manfred Lurker, *The Gods and Symbols of Ancient Egypt: An Illustrated Dictionary.* Lurker's spellings and dates remain speculative; but his book provided a recent reference guide for my decisions, although following it in every case proved to be impractical.

10

# 1

# Mythological Stories

At evening the waterlily closes its blossom and draws the bud far under the surface of the water; so far that it cannot even be reached by hand. In the morning the sun's rays draw it to the surface again, where it opens to full bloom. This cycle caused early Egyptians to associate the flower with the coming of the sun. One of the creation myths, which survives only in part, told that the world was a limitless dark sea before there was life. Out of this rose a large, luminous lotus bud which brought both light and perfume to the world. The lotus became a symbol for the sun which seemed to break forth from the chaos of dark water each morning. That the petals of the bloom radiated out from its center like shafts of sunlight probably added to the symbolism. The lotus was called "the redolent flower, the soul of Ra," and the great sun god was believed to hide inside the bloom. In the Book of the Dead, there is a spell which the dead person used in order to become a lotus flower: he thought of it as a symbol for rebirth since it came anew out of the depths each morning. The lotus became the political symbol for Upper Egypt and was included in most depictions of kings of that region, just as the papyrus became the symbol for Lower Egypt.

The myths of the lotus, a prominent Egyptian symbol from the ancient period down to modern times, are characteristic of the mythology of this ancient culture. Mysteries of nature which directly influenced daily life, especially the movement of the sun, were explained in stories that united man's wish to understand the origin of all things with the realities of political events. The theme of the lotus myth takes its place among the major subjects of Egyptian mythology: creation, daily renewal, rejuvenation of the soul—and politics.

Nearly two and a half thousand years have passed since Alexander the Great conquered Egypt, yet images from the myths of that ancient civilization continue to surface. In the 1970s, one of Bob Dylan's songs was named after the goddess Isis, the eternal mother. Tourists at the historic sites of Egypt buy reproductions of Thoth, Anubis, Bes, and scores of other ancient gods. The United States dollar depicts an eye and pyramid, Masonic borrowings from ancient Egypt; and numerous Egyptian companies (including the national airline, with its Horus logo) use names, faces and cartouches from the old mythology to promote their products and services. Ancient monuments from Egypt dot the cityscape of major urban centers in Europe. The contemporary writer Norman Mailer has used the myths of Egypt as the basis for his novel, *Ancient Evenings*.

What is the power of myth? The word itself comes from a Geek word meaning "story;" but myths as we know them are more than mere folktales: they are stories with a special significance for the culture which gave them birth. In his recent book *The Great Code: the Bible and Literature,* Northrop Frye describes myths as "stories that tell a society what is important for it to know, whether about its gods, its history, its laws, or its class structure."

The mythology of a particular group of people—what is important for them to know—is made up of interrelated and interwoven myths, although in preliterate times the mythology was probably not viewed as a whole. In fact, in most cases, if not all, the apparent unity of ancient mythology is the product of nineteenth- and twentieth-century writers.

In selecting these gods and stories from Egyptian mythology for retelling, I too may have created some appearance of unity in order to simplify a complex and often conflicting body of myths, most of which are not as well-known as, for example, their Greek counterparts which have been retold in popular form innumerable times. Egyptian mythology was unusually long-lasting. Its earliest records date from about 2345 B.C. in carvings at Sakkara, and some of the stories were still current several centuries into the Christian era.

Plate 1. Lotus

We cannot expect to find unity in a mythology that spanned over three thousand years. Moreover, there were many cult-centers, each with its own gods, such as Heliopolis, Memphis, Elephantine, Thebes. As each of these centers enjoyed its period of political ascendancy, it assimilated its own theology with some of the others in order to achieve dominance. This process brought many of the myths into general accord but left others in a state of conflict which was never resolved.

This book is therefore a compilation from many sources of tales concerning the sacred characters of ancient Egypt. The tales of these gods are full of fun and interest. They amuse and startle, as well as shed light on the workings of pre-philosophic minds. They not only give us a picture of an early society, but they also provide sparkling entertainment. They are full of the richness, vitality, earthiness and curiosity of a culture that produced some of the longest-lasting monuments known to man.

# 2

# The Great Ennead of Heliopolis

The Biblical book of Genesis tells us that when the King of Egypt wanted to reward Joseph for his faithful and wise service, he married him to the daughter of a priest of On. On was the biblical name for the place that the ancient Egyptians called Annu and the Greeks were to call Heliopolis, "city of the sun," because of its relation with the sun god Ra. It is the Greek name which survives. Today Heliopolis is one of the more fashionable suburbs of Cairo, some five miles or so from the downtown center; but in early history the priests of Ra had established Annu as the religious capital of Egypt. Through the centuries the priests built there an important temple to Ra, founded a college, and collected an important library. Tradition holds that the great Greek philosophers Solon, Thales, and Plato visited the College and that Plato actually studied there. Plutarch said that Pythagoras also came to Egypt, where he was much admired; he may even have used some of the Egyptian symbolism and occult teachings in his own work. Another legend says that a priest, Manetho, who wrote a history of Egypt for Ptolemy II in the third century B.C., did his research at the library in Heliopolis.

From the visit of the Ethiopian King Piankhi to Heliopolis in about 730 B.C., we have some record of what the town must have looked like. The temple was located on the 'high sand' north of the town; this apparently referred to a man-made hill supposed to

15

represent the primeval hill on which Ra arose at the creation. The temple was probably enclosed in a thick, high wall; and in the open court inside was the *benben* stone, a rude form of obelisk, which caught the sun's rays each morning to show that the sun god was in residence in his temple. At the base of the stone was the altar where kings left prodigious sacrifices in honor of the sun god; in the fifth dynasty there is record of a New Year's Day sacrifice of 100,600 meals of bread, beer, and cake, evidently intended for the god, his priests, and the royal court. Some sort of structure had been there from the fourth dynasty onwards, but major construction took place during the fifth dynasty when the large temple was built. Little evidence of this temple has so far been uncovered, but we can obtain some idea of it from ruins at Abu Gurob, whose temple, according to Cyril Aldred, was modeled on the one in Heliopolis. In addition to the walled enclosure, obelisk and altar, the followers of Ra also constructed a large mud-brick replica of Ra's solar boat and set it just outside the walls. Nearby was the fountain of the sun, which became a lake of considerable size. At the impressive entrance stood a pair of granite obelisks, each about sixty-five feet high, possibly erected by Sesostris I, who also renovated the old temple. The obelisks were capped with metal—probably gold or copper—in order to reflect the rays of the sun, which were supposed to fall on them before any of the other structures in the area. Today one of these stones is the only standing survivor of the grandeur of this once powerful shrine.

Later, during the flight of the Holy Family, Mary is supposed to have rested at On and is said to have washed her son's clothes at the fountain. Today little of ancient Heliopolis remains, but the mythology developed at Annu provides us with the most central of all Egyptian stories.

According to Siegfried Morenz, the theological system at Heliopolis evolved during the third to the fifth dynasties (roughly 2780-2300 B.C.) and dominated Egypt until the emergence of a mythology from Memphis around the fifth dynasty, at which time the two systems began to merge. The priests of Heliopolis spread the names of their gods throughout the country and found ways to assimilate many of the local gods from the rest of Egypt into the group worshipped along with Ra. From the fifth dynasty onward, the kings of Egypt took special care to associate themselves, either by bloodline

16

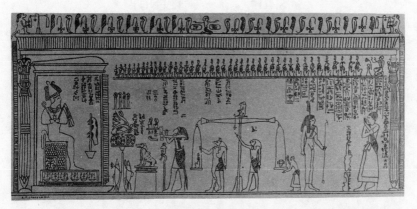

**Plate** 2.  Trial of a soul before the gods: one of the basic myths often mentioned in the text

or marriage, with Ra, the chief god of the Great Ennead (an ennead is a group of nine). The Great Ennead focussed on Ra as first principle, from whom the other gods evolved. Its family tree provides a visual overview of the complex interrelationships of the featured players:

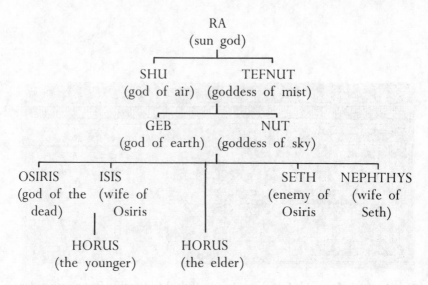

Actually neither the elder nor the younger Horus was properly a member of the Great Ennead, but since both play parts in its activities, they are placed here to show their relationship with the others. Horus the Elder was sometimes listed as a fifth child of Geb and Nut, and Horus the Younger was the famous son of Osiris and Isis who assumed the role of the dominant god after his father's death. The placement of Horus the Younger is a good example of how complex the mythologizing of Egypt was. Horus had been an important god in some regions to the south of Heliopolis before Ra came to dominate much of the land, but in this version of the myth he was positioned as Ra's descendant. The priests of Heliopolis eventually created a place in their system for this god who had to be reconciled with Ra.

In the story of creation that was developed in Heliopolis, the idea that the first of the gods evolved out of chaos and darkness and brought order to a disordered universe runs parallel to creation stories from many other cultures, including the Greek and Hebrew. In the

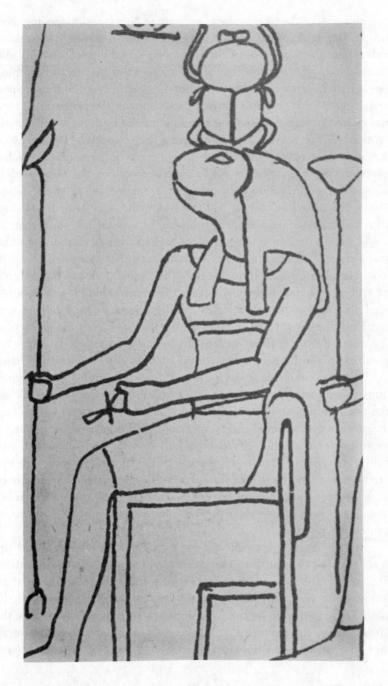

Plate 3. Nun

beginning were the primeval waters, named Nun (variant spelling: Nu) which, since they were unconscious and inanimate, were incapable of independent action. Out of the waters Ra raised himself on a hill and created himself. Ra says that at the moment of his creation nothing else existed, neither the heavens, nor the earth, nor the things upon earth. Until this moment he had lived alone in the primeval waters, where he developed in darkness and contained both male and female principles. For reasons that remain obscure to mortals, he conceived the idea of creation and willed his own physical existence. What happened next is open to some controversy, but the most widely accepted version follows the concept as expressed in the Pyramid Texts, which tell us that Ra was the god "who once came into being, who masturbated in On. He took his phallus in his grasp that he might create orgasm by means of it, and so were born the twins Shu and Tefnut." The exact details are hazy and what happened seems to have been anatomically possible only for a chief god, but Ra said that he embraced his own shadow during this remarkable act and "poured seed into my own mouth." His children were formed and he spat them out: Shu was to be the god of the air and Tefnut the goddess of the mist. Ra said that he "became from one god three gods." This act resulted in the immediate existence of light and dispersal of chaos.

While in the darkness of the Primeval Waters, Ra equipped himself with an eye, which he sent out to find Shu and Tefnut. When the eye returned and discovered that it had been replaced in Ra's face by another eye, it became very angry. Ra had to placate it by giving it more power than the second one, but then he was stuck with two eyes. He therefore made one the eye of the sun and the other the eye of the moon, and he turned the solar eye into a rearing cobra and used it to protect himself from his enemies. (The cobra was the symbol that kings afixed to their crowns in order to benefit from its protective powers.)

After creating himself and his two children Ra wept, and the tears that fell gave birth to mortal men and women. In the meantime Shu and Tefnut joined together as man and wife, and out of their union came Geb, the god of the earth, and Nut, the goddess of the sky. These two were locked in an embrace as they were born (like the Greeks later, the Egyptians gave their gods impressive sexual powers), and Shu had to come between them. He lifted Nut up into the area

20

Plate 4.  Ra

above the earth and lo! the universe as the ancient Egyptians knew it was formed. The sky and air hovered just above the earth and separated it from the heavens. It was Nut and Geb who then provided the universe with a population of gods and goddesses who were to be the dramatis personae of Egyptian mythology.

According to Plutarch, and Sir James Frazer's *The Golden Bough,* Ra actually considered Nut his wife. When he realized that she was enamored of Geb, he became furious and placed a curse on her that she should bear children in no month and no year. Nut turned for help to Thoth, the god of wisdom. Now Thoth had been playing at draughts with the moon and had beaten her badly enough to win one seventy-second part of every day. The Egyptian year consisted of three hundred and sixty days, but Thoth combined all his winnings into five whole days, which he then added to the regular calendar year. (This story explains why a piece of the moon appears to be missing for a time each month; and the Egyptians did in fact add five days to their calendar at the end of each year in order to bring it into accord with solar time.) These five days were not considered part of the regular year, and therefore Ra's curse on Nut did not apply to them. Nut took full advantage of this loophole, and on the first of the non-calendar days she gave birth to Osiris. On the second she bore horus the Elder, on the third Seth, on the fourth Isis, and on the fifth Nephthys. Thus the Great Ennead was created, and they became the source of all other life.

## RA

He was a version of the sun god, and Egyptian art most often represented him with the solar disk—a circle drawn over the head of deities associated with the sun. Frequently Ra was depicted with the body of a man and head of a hawk. Ra's human body and hawk head were often similar to depictions of the god Horus, the difference being that Horus wore a crown on his head while Ra wore the disk of the sun encircled by a cobra. (The association with the cobra suggested his fierce and destructive nature, which will become apparent in the story of the destruction of mankind to be told in the next chapter.) Ra was usually shown holding a scepter in one hand and an ankh in the other.

Plate 5.   Osiris holding an ankh

The ankh is one of the most popular Egyptian symbols, both in ancient art and in modern reproductions. A symbol of life, it is shown in many drawings held by a god in front of the king's nostrils, so that the breath of eternal life would enter his body. On some temple walls in Upper Egypt the ankh was used as a sign for water in rituals of purification. Here, the king would stand between two gods (one of whom was usually Thoth) as they poured over him a stream of libations represented by ankhs. The ankh was also used decoratively on thrones and platforms for kings and gods. Its origins are obscure: some believe it was a rendition of a sandal strap, or a knot. Guides in Egypt today like to tell tourists that the circle at the top represents the female sexual organ, the stump at the bottom the male organ, and the crossed line, the children of the union. This interpretation may have a long tradition, but scholarly research has so far failed to verify it.)

The character of Ra as seen in the Book of the Dead is described in a hymn:

You rise, you rise, you shine, you shine, you who are crowned king of
     the gods.
You are the lord of heaven,
You are the lord of the earth;
You are the creator of those who dwell in the heights and of those
     who dwell in the depths.
You are the God One who came into being in the beginning of time.
You did create the earth, you did fashion man,
You did make the watery abyss of the sky,
You did form Hapi [the Nile].
You did create the watery abyss,
And you do give life to all that therein is.
You have knit together the mountains,
You have made mankind and the beasts of the field to come into
     being,
You have made the heavens and the earth.
Worshipped be you whom Maat [the goddess of truth and justice]
     embraces at morn and at eve.
You travel across the sky with heart swelling with joy....

24

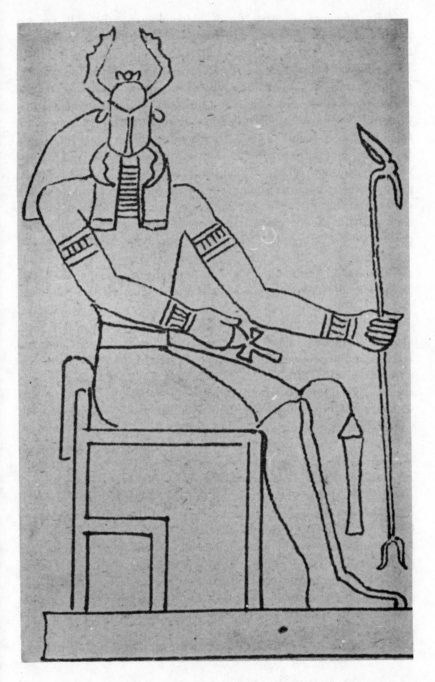

Plate 6. Khepri

Ra appeared in other forms, depending on the role he was playing at the moment: "I am Khepri in the morning, and Ra at noonday, and Atum in the evening." Khepri (variant spelling: Khepera) was the god of the scarab beetle, and in Egypt the worship of the scarab was much older than the worship of Ra. That Ra became associated with Khepri and the scarab is further evidence that the priests of Ra were able to assimilate their more recent god with the established ones. This particular association, however, had a fascinating biological origin. Ancient Egyptians had observed that the scarab beetle laid its egg in dung and then pushed it around on the ground until it became a ball. The Egyptians imagined that the ball symbolized the sun because it was round, gave off heat, and was the source of life, and because it seemed to represent the self-creative powers of the sun god. They then pictured the sun being pushed across the sky by a giant beetle. Eventually this imagery became associated with death and rebirth too, since it appeared that the beetle had died and was born again when the larva emerged from the ball.

When the sun god assumed the character of Khepri, he was usually depicted in human form with a scarab either on top of or in place of his head. Like Ra, he was most often carrying an ankh and scepter, and he was considered a god of creation, since the beetle was most often observed in the act of creating itself anew. Khepri was also associated with the resurrection of the body, since that was what seemed to be happening when the scarab was born. This fact explains why Egyptians placed the scarab in tombs and on bodies of the dead. This, then, was the form of Ra in the morning.

He took his own shape at mid-day, but in the evening he assumed the form of Atum (variant spellings: Temu, Tem, Atem). Atum is one of the oldest forms of the sun god to have been revered by ancient Egyptians, and it was in this form that Ra was supposed to have created the universe out of chaos. In temple drawings he was always represented as being fully human, without an animal head. He was especially revered because of his association with the souls of the dead. He rode in the solar boat during the final hours of daylight, preparing to fight his opponents in the night. It was believed that souls recently released from their bodies waited at the beginning of the Valley of the Tuat (the underworld) for the solar boat, which meant that they came aboard just as the sun went down into the

Plate 7.  Atum

underworld—the time when the pilot of the solar boat was Atum, the form of Ra in the evening.

In addition to Ra's manifestations as Khepri and Atum, he was linked with numerous other gods throughout his long reign. Very early he was linked with Horus to form the assimilated god Herakhty, or Horus as the morning sun; it was this relationship that led Egyptians to depict Ra with a hawk's head. During the Middle Kingdom, when Amun and his Theban priests dominated Egyptian religion, Ra was assimilated with this god from the South to form Amun-Ra, whose worship in Thebes (now called Luxor) led to the building of the Temple of Karnak, one of the most imposing religious structures made by man.

The curious student of Ra today will find scant remains of the once considerable worship of this god. His character was so much assimilated with those of other gods, or other gods so often acquired his attributes, that only rarely now do we find relics that depict him singly. Of the mighty temple at Heliopolis, little remains now but the single obelisk. The exact date of the destruction of this temple is unknown, but some time before the Christian era little remained except stones that were used for buildings elsewhere in Egypt.

South of Cairo the worship of the sun god almost always involved another god, usually Amun. Walls of the tomb of Seti I, one of the most impressively carved tombs in the Valley of the Kings, depict the myth of the destruction of mankind under Ra's orders (see Chapter Three). Other royal tombs there contain a list of seventy-five Praises of Ra which reveal his character, as in this example: "Praise be unto you, O Ra, you exalted power, who enter into the hidden place of Anubis [god of death]; behold [your] body is Khepri." Even further south at Abu Simbel, Ra was again worshipped in combination with other gods; the Great Temple of Ramesses II was dedicated to Ra-Herakhty.

Ra was also depicted in the papyrus scrolls that make up what we call the Book of the Dead. They contain hymns and prayers to Ra in his various forms, as well as numerous beautiful drawings of him. The papyri are in libraries in Europe now, but they can be consulted in published works, some of which are listed in the bibliography of this book. Drawn vignettes in the Papyrus of Ani show Ra as a falcon-headed man wearing the solar disk while riding in his boat. Other

28

Plate 8. Shu

drawings show Khepri and Atum in the solar boat. In the Papyrus of Hunefer Ra is shown with a full falcon body, wearing the solar disk encircled by a cobra. The god is honored by Hunefer and his wife and adored by seven baboons (presumably one for each day of the week). Baboons chatter so much at the rising of the sun that the ancient Egyptians began to associate them with the sun god, an association that can clearly be seen on the face of the Great Temple at Abu Simbel. The same papyrus also contains an important representation of Ra as the cat attacking Apophis with a knife, the story of which is told in the following chapter. Hunefer identified himself with those who, like the cat, protect Ra from his enemies. The Papyrus of Anhai contains a beautiful drawing of Nun holding the solar boat. Inside at the center of the boat is not Ra but a scarab pushing the solar disk skyward, where it is received by Osiris and Nut. Watching the rising sun from advantageous positions inside the boat are seven deities, one of whom has a falcon head and may well be Ra.


## SHU

One of the spells from the Coffin Texts had Shu describing his own attributes:

I am Shu, whom Atum created on the day that he himself appeared.
He did not form me in a womb nor shape me in an egg,
I was not conceived by any manner of conception,
But my father Atum spat me forth with the spittle of his mouth, me
    and my sister Tefnut.
She emerged behind me when I was enveloped in the breath of life
    that came from the throat of the phoenix,
      on the day that Atum appeared
      in the infinity, the nothing, the darkness and shapelessness.
I am Shu, Father of the gods—
    which was when Atum sent out his single eye to seek me and my
    sister Tefnut.
I am he who made the darkness light for her when she found me as a
    man upholding.

We have already seen that the most authoritative form of the creation story claimed that Shu and Tefnut were created as result of Ra's masturbation and his spitting out the children from his mouth. Although other myths offered different versions (suggesting that Shu was the son of Hathor or Iusaset), these left unexplained both the origin of these goddesses and their union with Ra at a time when he was supposed to be the only power in existence. A Victorian scholar, E.A. Wallis Budge, shocked by the crudity of the masturbation story, which he believed to be the original one, suggested that its originators must have been semi-savage, possibly from Libya; and that later Egyptians, embarrassed by the story, substituted the other tales that were less offensive but more convoluted. His theory is given little credence today but remains a charming example of nineteenth-century British propriety.

Shu was usually represented with completely human traits. On his head he wore an ostrich feather known for both its size and lightness, an appropriate emblem for the god of the air. He was lord of the space between earth and sky, and he supported the sky, holding her up with his hands. He represented the light that brought an end to the darkness which reigned alongside chaos in the time before creation. He had also been seen as a personification of the wind that blew out of the north, an important wind in Egypt since it came from the Mediterranean up the Nile, cooling houses in summer and driving feluccas (single-masted sail boats) on their voyages. Another of the spells from the Coffin Texts had Shu claim that he was of all the gods "the captain of the crew,... the strongest and most vigorous of the Divine Band." He saw himself as the companion and assistant to Ra. He has been compared to "the dawn breeze which announces the coming of the sun."

Shu was frequently depicted in amulets and in porcelain figures. In Pharaonic drawings, however, he is most typically shown separating his children, Geb and Nut, from each other and holding his daughter up as the sky.

## TEFNUT

Shu and his twin sister were said by the Book of the Dead to have but one soul between them. Tefnut, Shu's female principle, was usually

31

considered the goddess of mist, the source of moisture in the newly created universe. In the story of **creation** we saw that the eye of Ra which Shu and Tefnut brought with them played a crucial role, but an additional part of the story says that Nun made for Ra a second eye, an act which made the first eye angry. Ra had to use all his diplomacy to keep both eyes content and, as a result, divided their duties. One eye became responsible for the daylight hours and had considerable power and splendor; the second accepted responsibility for the hours of night and also had splendor but less power. This is one version of the myth of the creation of the sun and moon, and often Tefnut was associated with the moon, Ra's lunar eye. Later this clear distinction became blurred, and Tefnut was at times identified with the solar eye as well, sometimes being called "the lady of flame."

In her role as the eye of Ra she played a part in a very interesting myth that has been pieced together from references at the temples of Edfu and Dendera. Tefnut became very angry with her father and left Annu for Nubia (the area now covered by Lake Nasser) in a very bad mood. There she took on the form of an angry lioness and became the terror of the neighborhood, attacking both men and animals. Dragon-like, she blew smoke and fire from her nostrils and eyes and fed upon the flesh and blood of her victims. Ra missed his daughter and perhaps believed that he could use her new-found ferocity to his own advantage against his enemies, so he sent Shu and Thoth as his emissaries to ask her to return home. Thoth, disguised as a baboon—which may account for his later association with the animal—found her first and tried to persuade her that Egypt was a much more civilized place than the wilds of the Nubian desert. In Egypt, he said, her worshippers would serve up to her on altars the game she was now having to run down and kill for herself. He described the festivals and joy that characterized Egypt and generally made the case for a superior life there. Shu finally caught his brother up and joined Thoth in encouraging his sister and mate to return to Egypt. The two gods ultimately prevailed on Tefnut to go home, and her return trip became a triumphant progress through the Egyptian villages. The goddess was accompanied by Nubian musicians, clowns, and baboons; the people turned out to rejoice in her presence, and wild drunkenness accompanied the festivals in her honor. As she progressed through the villages, she lost her ferocity and became

Plate 9.   Tefnut

much kinder and gentler. The myth was presented as an explanation of the civilizing power of culture: while she was in the desert, she was wild and uncontrollable, but when she returned to the niceties of civilization, she calmed down and became a good citizen. The myth also reflected ancient ideas about the sun and moon. As the eye—whether she represented at this moment the sun or the moon makes little difference—her absence caused the absence of light, and the people became afraid. Her return indicated the victory of light over darkness and was a signal for rejoicing. This story is one version of the return of the eye of the god, a central theme too in the Osiris-Horus-Seth myth.

Tefnut was sometimes presented in the drawings in the shape of a woman wearing the solar disk encircled by a cobra. While it is usually assumed that her disk represented the sun, there was nothing about it that might not also have represented the moon. At other times she had a woman's body and lioness' head, and elsewhere she was depicted simply as a lioness. Not much is known about her role in mythology, but she did have a place in the court of judgment during the trials of recently departed souls before the gods. Her role was minor, but the papyri of both Ani and Hunefer contain vignettes in which she sits as judge.

## GEB

Perhaps the best known activity of Shu and Tefnut was to give birth to two children, Geb and Nut; Shu was then responsible for separating the two and creating from them the earth and sky. Geb was the god of the earth. The Coffin Texts told of Ra's boredom; the chief god complained he had been too long at leisure, and had grown weary of it: "If the earth were alive," Ra thought, "it would cheer my heart and enliven my bosom." So the earth was created both to make Ra's life more interesting and to give him a place to rest when he became weary.

The usual depiction of Geb was a male figure wearing on his head either the white crown of Lower Egypt or a goose. The goose was his sign and he was known in the Book of the Dead as the Great Cackler.

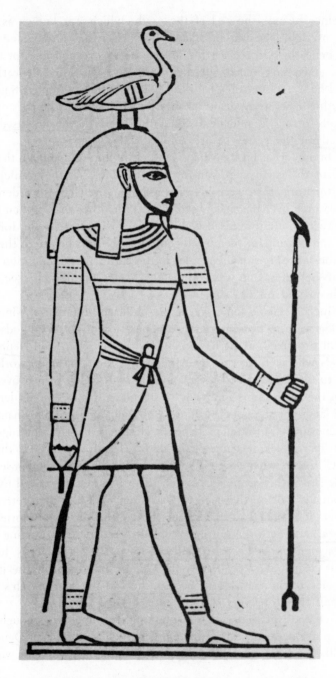

Plate 10.  Geb

Since he was the god of the earth, which was known as "the house of Geb," he was involved with life on the surface and with death beneath. On the earth's surface he was responsible for trees, plants, and seeds which put their roots into his soil. Beneath the ground he was responsible for dead bodies buried in tombs. Since he was intimate with the dead, he was shown in many papyri as one of the gods sitting in judgment when the heart of the deceased was weighed on the scales before Anubis and Thoth.

On one occasion Ra called Geb before him to complain that the snakes of the earth were causing him trouble. As they came from Geb's territory, they were his responsibility, and Geb was ordered to keep a watch over the snakes and inform the other gods of their plans and activities. Ra promised Geb help in this matter, in the form of spells and charms for men intelligent enough to make use of them to draw the snakes out of their holes in the earth. The assumption must be that Geb did as he was commanded, since nothing else seems to have been said on the subject.

Much of Geb's fame lay in the children he fathered, since his offspring were to become the next generation of powerful gods. He and Nut produced, as we have seen, Osiris, Isis, Seth, and Nephthys, the gods who were to rule over the earth, skies, and underworld. A hymn to Osiris described the manner in which Geb turned over the rule of the earth to his son: Geb "assigned to [Osiris] the leadership of the lands for the good of affairs. He put this land in his hand, its water, its air, its verdure, all its herds, all things that fly, all things that flutter, its reptiles, its game of the desert, legally conveyed to the son of Nut." Later, when Osiris was confronted by enemies and in serious trouble, his father came to his aid. The Pyramid Texts tell us that Geb put his foot on the head of Osiris' enemy, who then retreated. Another document placed Geb in the conflict between Horus (his grandson) and Seth (his son). He tried to separate his warring heirs and assigned Upper Egypt to Seth and Lower Egypt to Horus, but he made it clear in a speech before the Great Ennead that he was giving the choice territory to Horus because he was the son of Geb's first-born and therefore very dear to him.

Geb and Nut were accorded no temple of their own, though Geb was apportioned parts of major temples, such as the one at Dendera. Most likely he was chiefly worshipped at Heliopolis, where he was the

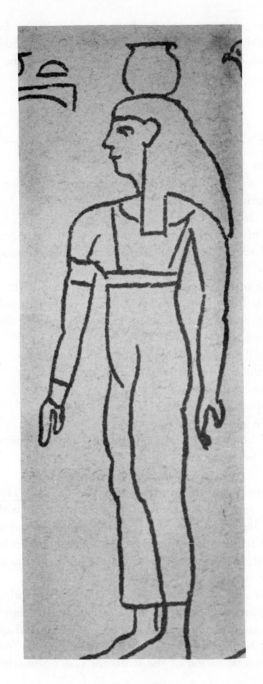

Plate 11.  Nut

ground on which the temple to Ra was built. In the Tutankhamun collection at the Egyptian Museum, there is a gilded wooden statue of Geb that had been placed in the tomb to protect the boy-king.

## NUT

The Pyramid Texts contained a long poem spoken by Geb to his wife:

O Nut! You became a spirit
You waxed mighty in the belly of your mother Tefnut before you
    were born.
How mighty is your heart!
You stirred in the belly of your mother in the name of Nut,
You are indeed a daughter more powerful than her mother...
O great One who has become the sky!
You have the mastery, you have filled every place with your beauty,
The whole earth lies beneath you, you have taken possession thereof,
    you have enclosed the whole earth and everything therein within
    your arms...
As Geb I shall impregnate you in your name of sky,
I shall join the whole earth to you in every place.
O high above the earth!
You are supported upon your father Shu,
But you have power over him,
He so loved you that he placed himself—and all things
    beside—beneath you.

This love-poem contained the essence of Nut's character: she was the sky who shared a very special relationship with the earth beneath her. She became pregnant by her husband and was supported by her father. Each day the sun god passed through her on his voyage in the solar boat, and the stars were part of her being, as children are part of their mother.

Nut was almost always depicted as a woman with remarkable physical proportions. Most of the drawings showed her nude, with large breasts and detailed anatomy. She was pretty and appealing. If she wore any headdress, it was a vase of water, and her name derived from the phonetic sound of the word for vase. Sometimes she was

Plate 12. Shu separating Geb and Nut

shown standing in a sycamore tree, her symbol, pouring out water to purify the souls of the dead.

The myth that was basic to her explains her relationship with the sun. Nut was supposed to give birth daily to her son, the sun. He then passed over her body until he reached her mouth, whereupon she ate him, and he disappeared until it was time for him to be born again the next morning. This myth was frequently represented in Pharaonic ceiling paintings, such as that of the temple at Dendera or the tomb of Ramesses VI at Luxor. Here she is shown nude; her limbs and trunk so extraordinarily long that her body covers—in some painting—the outline of three edges of the ceiling. Her hands begin in one corner and her arms take up the length of one wall. The second and third wall-lengths are taken up by her body and legs respectively, with her feet reaching to the end of the third wall. The sun, in the form of a ball, is depicted rolling over her body from the point of birth to her mouth, where it was to be eaten. Elsewhere, Nut's ceiling appearance is more symbolic: in the Pyramid of Unas at Sakkara it is made up of thousands of small stars, creating a sky-like background for the hieroglyphics which form part of the Pyramid Texts.·

Another version of this myth is again concerned with Nut eating her own children. This story tells how the stars followed Ra into the mouth of their mother, and disappeared during the daytime. Geb became angry at the thought of his wife eating her children and quarreled with her, comparing her to "the sow that eats her piglets." Her father, however, intervened and sent a message to Geb not to be angry. Shu insisted that the eating of the children each morning assured that they would be born again that evening and would therefore survive safely.

Nut was often connected with Hathor, the cow goddess. In one myth Ra had fallen into serious trouble with the residents of earth. Nun advised him to mount the back of Nut in her cow form and ride away through the sky to escape the anger of the humans. In typical drawings of this story, the boats of Ra can be seen beside her front legs where they join her body, and also to the rear beside her udder. Ra himself rides in the foremost of the two boats. Nut's belly is lined with stars, and Shu stands under her supporting the sky. This one scene illustrates four different concepts of the sky held by ancient

Egyptians: the woman, the cow, the ocean (through which the boats sail), and the ceiling over Shu which must be supported.

The Pyramid Texts were full of prayers to Nut to provide protection for the dead, since the gods flying daily through the sky in their boat were under her protection, as were the souls of the dead. As a sign of this role for Nut, many sarcophagi have her image carved on the undersides of their lids. While the dead person lies there eternally, he looks up at the personification of the sky. As a result, one of her many names was "the great protectress." Examples of this image of Nut can be found in both the Egyptian Museum and the British Museum.

Nut's greatest role, however, was as the mother of the main body of gods in the Great Ennead. Myths told us that she and Geb, the earth, entered into an embrace each night; and the Pyramid Texts told us that the earth was an island that lay between the legs of Nut. The inevitable result was that she gave birth to the major gods of the next generation. For this Nut was known in the Coffin Texts as "she with the braided hair who gave birth to the gods."

In her capacity as the sky, the protector of men and gods, the ocean through which Ra made his daily journey, and the mother of the gods, Nut was one of the most highly revered of the Great Ennead. She was probably depicted in more different scenes and myths than any of the others, yet her personal power was small. She served and protected others more powerful than herself.

## OSIRIS

Of all the gods of Egypt Osiris was the best known; a famous hymn to him from the Book of the Dead captured his essence:

> Glory be to you, O Osiris... the great god within Abydos, king of eternity and lord of everlastingness, the god who passes through millions of years in your existence. You are the eldest son of the womb of Nut, you were engendered by Geb, the Ancestor of the gods, you are the lord of the crowns of the North and the South, and of the lofty white crown. As prince of the gods and of men, you have received the crook and the whip and the dignity of

41

your divine fathers. Let your heart which is in the mountain of [the underworld] be content, for your son Horus is established upon your throne. You are crowned the lord of Mendes and ruler in Abydos. Through you the world waxes green in triumph.

Osiris is perhaps the most easily recognized of the gods. He was always dressed in white mummy's clothes; he wore a beard and held in his crossed arms the crook, the flail (whip), and sometimes the scepter—all signs of authority and power. Most often he was depicted as the judge of the dead person's soul. He was shown either standing on the platform throne of Maat (depicted as a shallow rectangle) or seated upon a throne floating on water out of which sprouted lotus flowers. On his head Osiris wore either the white crown of Lower Egypt or the atef crown, which was a combination of the white crown and two white plumes. The color of his skin helps to identify his qualities: sometimes it was painted white like a mummy, sometimes black to suggest death, and at times green to symbolize vegetation and resurrection.

Some scholars believe that Osiris may have been an actual human ruler early in civilization, but it is fairly certain that in prehistoric times Osiris became a minor fertility god associated with Anedjti, the chief god of the Delta village of Busiris. From Anedjti he took the crook and flail as symbols of power. In this form he apparently had the character of a dangerous god, and some suggestions of this trait—the crook and flail, for example—survived into later times. Sometime before the historic period began and Lower and Upper Egypt were united into one country, his image was transformed into that of a kind ruler who acted as guide to the underworld. His fame spread from the Delta into Upper Egypt and eventually Abydos became the center of his worship, although he was respected and worshipped throughout the country.

According to the myths, Osiris had become very successful as a ruler and leader on earth, teaching human beings to give up barbaric practices and to learn to grow grain. His brother Seth grew jealous and killed him by sealing his body in a casket and throwing it into the Nile. Isis, Osiris' wife and sister, sought the body of her husband, but even after she found it, Seth continued to plague her. This time he

42

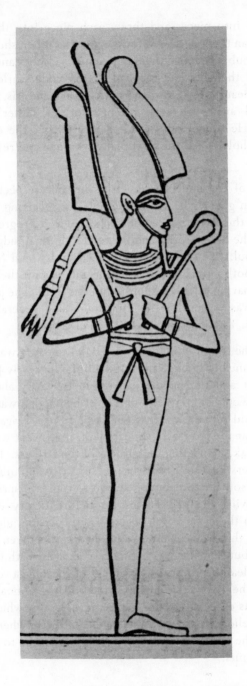

Plate 13. Osiris

cut the body into pieces and threw each piece into the river. Isis faithfully began the long search for the pieces. When she found them, Thoth and Anubis wrapped them in mummy's clothes and restored his shape; Osiris then became the god of the underworld.

In the meantime, Horus, the son of Osiris and Isis, had grown to maturity and sworn to seek revenge for his father's death and mutilation. He sought out Seth and they fought the epic battle of Egyptian mythology. Horus eventually won and the rest of the gods made peace.

As god of the underworld, Osiris became respected above all other Egyptian gods. He was responsible for receiving reports from other gods of the recently dead person's soul as it progressed through the trials of the underworld, and for rendering final judgment on the fate of the soul. He was usually attended by Isis and Nephthys and assisted by Thoth and Horus, who spent only part of their time in the underworld, having earthly responsibilities as well. The jackal-headed god Anubis was responsible for embalming and generally preparing the body and, as such, was Osiris's chief assistant.

Before the recent building of the High Dam at Aswan, the waters of the Nile annually flooded the entire river valley. By June the land had dried out and the people had begun to worry about the next flood: when would it come? Would it bring enough water this year? Then about mid-July the water would begin to rise, irrigating the low-lying areas near the river bed. In early fall, if all went well, the flood reached its peak, inundating the gardens of the farmers. By winter the receding waters had left a layer of silt, rich in minerals which fertilized the soil for the coming season's crops. In spring the crops would be growing, ready for harvest just before the dry season in early summer when the cycle began again. Osiris became identified with the river and the growing crops. He had earlier been viewed as a fertility god, but later he was naturally associated with the river that had been his deathbed on two occasions. He became a vegetable god, symbolic of the river's life-giving force and the annual renewal of crops. He was especially connected with the grains which nourished the gods of Heliopolis as well as the people of earth; when turned into liquid form, the grains became beer which was sacred to the gods and joy-giving to men.

44

Many festivals were held in his honor, since his worship extended from the Delta to the first cataract in the south; a Greco-Roman text on the walls of the temple at Dendera described an ancient ritual performed annually in Osiris' honor as early as the Middle Kingdom. At the time when the flood was at its height, the Feast of Khoiak began with the celebration of an effigy of the dead god, cast in gold and filled with a mixture of sand and grain. As the waters were receding and grain was being planted in the land, the effigy was watered daily. Then for three days it was floated on the waters of the Nile, and on the twenty-fourth day of the month of Khoiak it was placed in a coffin and laid in a grave. On the thirtieth day, the effigy was actually buried. This seven-day delay represented the god's seven-day gestation in the womb of Nut, his mother. On the last day, the king and priests raised a djed pillar—a phallic symbol of the rejuvenation and strength of Osiris—as a sign that he had been born again and that the land would be fertile for yet another year.

Since Osiris was the god of the underworld, he was not worshipped in the same sense as were the sun gods, but numerous temples were built in his honor. His chief cult sites were Abydos, with its remarkable temples built by Seti I and his son Ramesses II; Dendera, with the text of the ritual mentioned above; and Philae, where Osiris was revered in the Temple of Isis. Many of the tombs and temples of Upper Egypt contain depictions of Osiris as the god of the underworld and as the god of renewed life. A large number of statuary representations of Osiris from these sites have found their way to museums around the world.

Much of what we know about Osiris, however, comes in textual form. The Pyramid Texts, the Coffin Texts, and the Book of the Dead contain the basis of our knowledge about Osiris' role in the treatment of the dead. The Book of the Dead's vignettes provide us with drawings of the god that are especially vivid (and often reproduced). The basic myth of the murder of Osiris and the search for his body, as well as the war between Seth and Horus, is told in Plutarch's essay "Isis and Osiris" dating from the first century after Christ.

One of the best-known of the ancient goddesses, Isis represents the archetype of wifely love and devoted motherhood. Her life as the wife of Osiris was pleasant until Seth's jealousy led him to murder his elder brother and to persecute his widow. Isis mourned her husband and located his body. She hid it from his vindictive brother and gave birth to Horus, who was to avenge his father's death and succeed him as chief god on earth. Seth feared the powers of his nephew and sought his death too, so Isis had to hide and protect her son until he was old enough to take care of himself. Her ordeals, and the faithfulness with which she followed her duty earned her the title of "Great Mother."

The love she bore her husband is beautifully expressed in a lament she sang for him after his death:

I am seeking after love:
Behold me existing in the city, great are its walls:
I grieve for your love for me—
Come you only, now that you have departed!
Behold your son, who caused Seth to retreat from destruction!
Hidden am I among the plants, and concealed is your son that he
    cannot answer you, while this great calamity remains!
Yet concerning you—
There is no likeness of your flesh left:
I follow you alone and surround the plants, each of which holds
    danger for your son,—
Lo, I, a woman, in front of all.

Isis' behavior to those about her was full of contradictory passions. On one hand, she could be ruthless in the pursuit of her husband's body. The king of Byblos offered the protection of his home and the help of his empire in recovering the body; her anguish, however, led to the deaths of two of his sons—horrible repayment for his friendship. In another myth she inflicted great pain on Ra, her great grandfather, in order to gain the power of his secret name; and she called on the other gods to bring total destruction on her enemies. Yet on the other hand when she saw Seth, her husband's murderer,

Plate 14.  Isis

about to be defeated in a battle she had ordered, she took pity on him and used her magic to permit his escape, a deed which rightly earned her the anger of her son.

Her power was often the result of her use of magic. She learned magical charms from Thoth in order to restore life to Osiris, and she practiced them later when Horus was bitten by Seth's scorpions. Throughout her life she used her magic on both friend and foe, and this secret knowledge gave her the reputation as a great healer of the sick, which lasted into the Christian era.

The usual drawing or statue of Isis showed her with human features. On her head she wore at different periods a vulture headdress, the horns of Hathor with a solar disk between them, or the throne. This last symbol, the throne, evolved from the sound of her name and associated her with kingly authority. She was sometimes identified by an amulet, called the Blood of Isis now, but called the *thet* by the ancient Egyptians. This charm was made of a red, semi-precious stone and placed in coffins to provide the dead with the power of the goddess who had raised her own husband and son from the dead. It resembles the ankh with its arms folded down and was often drawn alongside the djed pillar, the symbol of Osiris. The nineteenth-century scholar Wallis Budge suggested that the shape of the amulet resulted from the identification of Isis as the universal mother, and was a stylised representation of the vagina and uterus.

In the Book of the Dead Isis was usually depicted standing immediately behind Osiris, and alongside her sister Nephthys; the two goddesses provide support for their brother in his role as supreme judge of the dead. The vignettes also show the feminine pair as vultures guarding the bier on which rests the body of the dead person who has now assumed the characteristics of Osiris.

One of the most common depictions of Isis was of her nursing her son. This scene—in statuary, wall paintings, and papyri—sometimes showed other gods, such as Thoth, in attendance bringing gifts to the mother and child. The resemblance of Isis and her son to the Madonna and child was observed early in the Christian era and probably helped ease the way for the early acceptance of Christianity along the Nile.

The most important shrine to Isis is the Temple of Philae, on an island on the lake between the two dams at Aswan. This beautiful temple, one of those moved to preserve it from the rising waters,

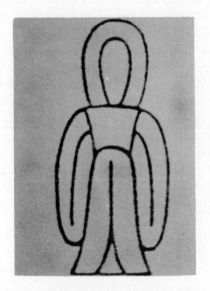

Plate 15.  Blood of Isis

associated Isis with the Nile and reaffirms some scholars' notion that in the most ancient days Isis was corn goddess in consort with her husband, the corn god. The largest of the temples here was built by Nectanebo I and later renovated by Ptolemy II, which makes it more recent than some of the other important temples to the north.

At Luxor Isis was represented in the Temple of Luxor, where she watches over Khnum as he molds a child on his potter's wheel in the Birth Room. Across the river in the tomb of Seti I, she and Nephthys provided special protection for the king who through death has become a god. She was distinctly represented in the treasures of Tutankhamun found in Luxor's Valley of the Kings and now residing in the Egyptian Museum. This museum contains many additional representations of Isis, including pieces from Abydos and Sakkara.

Outside Egypt Isis is probably the most famous of the Egyptian gods. Her powers were well known in Greece and Rome, thanks especially to Plutarch, who featured her in one of his books and who saw similarities with the Greek Artemis and Roman Diana. Palestine and other countries of the Middle East were hospitable to her, and her fame has lasted into modern times.

## SETH

All in all, the activities of the Great Ennead as a family rank them high with other historical and fictional families renowned for their corrupt and evil ways. Various members of the Great Ennead were at one time or another guilty of drunkenness, theft, incest, torture, matricide and mass murder. But every family needs a black sheep and every story needs a villain. In Egyptian mythology this role is given to Seth, whose misdeeds make those of the rest of his family look innocent by comparison.

The worship of Seth in Upper Egypt is quite ancient, and in the earliest times he was considered a beneficent god who assisted the dead. When his worshippers came in conflict with the cult of Horus somewhat later, they lost the political battles and his influence declined. The followers of Horus demoted Seth to a god of evil and ordered his shrines and images to be destroyed. Through the major part of Egyptian mythology Seth therefore represented evil, and in the

Plate 16. Seth

Egyptian view of a universe made up of a duality of evil and good, Seth played an important role in his opposition to the good gods. In this role he was to be defeated, even maimed, in battle; but he was never killed or eliminated, for his power was too great and of too much use to other gods. Much like Milton's Lucifer, he is a fascinating and compelling incarnation of evil, the manifestation of a recognized and necessary component of human behavior, and ultimately an agent of other gods who ironically accomplish their good through him. Most of the myths concerned with Seth depict him in this role.

The Pyramid Texts credited Seth with a violent nature from the moment of his birth: "You whom the pregnant goddess brought forth when you clove the night in twain—you are invested in the form of Seth, who broke out in violence." Early in his career Seth used his fierceness in behalf of other gods. He was placed in the front of the solar boat in order to fight off the enemies of Ra. In particular he was responsible for successfully defeating Apophis nightly with the curse: "Back, Villain! Plunge into the depths of the Abyss, into the place where your father ordained that you should be destroyed! Keep far away from this station of Ra, at whom you should tremble."

Eventually, however, his jealousy at the success of his older brother Osiris led him to murder the brother and persecute Isis in an attempt to take over the empire of the god of corn and vegetation. In the many different texts from the period, there were varying stories which placed Seth in combat to gain power for himself. The earliest of the stories told of the battle as a simple contest between day and night. A later story personified that idea: it showed Ra and Seth locked in combat, with Seth attempting to prevent the sun from rising each morning. In this version, strangely enough, Seth was associated with Apophis and attacked the solar boat he had earlier defended. His weapons were clouds, mists, rains, and darkness—a mythical explanation of natural phenomena which obscure the sun. In the third version of the conflict, Seth was pitted against his brother Osiris in an attempt to take over his powers. Finally, in the fourth version, Seth fought his nephew Horus the Younger in a battle that began with Horus' attempt to avenge his father's death, and ended as a fight for the territory once controlled by Osiris.

As the personification of sin and evil during this later period, Seth was god of storms and winds and was particularly associated with the desert, which was thought of as a place of death. One myth identified him with the sun as it set in the evening, and another related how he stole the fading light from the sun god, causing untold evil and harm. Thoth, the lunar god, brought renewed light with the rising of the moon, but Seth fought him too for the light of this heavenly body. Using storms, winds, earthquakes, and eclipses, Seth was able at times to gain a brief advantage over the sun and moon, but Ra and Thoth always won in the end.

The result of these character traits was that the Egyptians, as Plutarch recorded, held Seth "in the greatest contempt, and do all they can to vilify and affront him." At various times during the year specific rituals were observed to keep him from gaining power over light and vegetation. At one point a black pig (an animal often associated with Seth) was brutally cut into pieces upon a sand altar built on the river bank. At another time a model of a serpent was hacked to pieces. At another festival, recently captured birds and fish representing the god were trampled underfoot, to the chant: "You shall be cut into pieces, and your members shall be hacked asunder, and each of you shall consume the other: thus Ra triumphs over all his enemies... ."

Sometimes, however, Seth's ferocity was respected. Kings in the Ramesses cycle took him as their patron during the nineteenth and twentieth dynasties, and the name Seti of several of the kings—including the father of Ramesses II—was derived from the name of the god.

Herodotus told a story of the time Seth went to visit his mother Nut at the temple at Papremis. He had grown up elsewhere and the guards of the temple did not know him. When they refused him admission, he went to a nearby town, raised an army to storm the walls of the temple, and succeeded in forcing his way in. Herodotus said that in later years a ceremony was performed at the temple to commemorate the event. One group of priests carried a small, gold-plated wooden statue of Seth on a four-wheeled cart. They tried to gain admission to the temple but were denied it by another band of priests. A mock battle ensued in which thousands of men engaged each other with clubs. Herodotus believed that some were killed even though he had been assured that all this was done as part of a religious festival.

The physical form given to Seth was often that of a human body with the head of an animal. (Today the animal is called the Seth Animal because it is not otherwise identifiable.) The nose looked rather like that of a camel or an ass, and it had a tail that stood straight up and forked at the end. Some scholars think it might have been some sort of desert animal which was hunted to extinction at an early period, but others identify it as an aardvark, canine, or some other surviving creature. In truth it does not look quite like any animal we know today. At times Seth was simply portrayed in animal form without the human body. He was also associated with the serpent, ass, antelope, pig, hippopotamus, crocodile, and fish. Seth was a red god. His domain was the red desert, and only red oxen were sacrificed to him. Red-haired men were distrusted as his representatives on earth. He was married to Nephthys and their child was Anubis, the jackal-headed god of death, although there is some question of his paternity. After Seth's murder of Osiris, however, Nephthys was usually depicted as supporting Isis against Seth.

In the Valley of the Kings, Seth can be seen pouring libations over Seti I in his tomb, placing the crown on the head of Ramesses II, and teaching the young Thothmes III to use a bow and arrow. He was remembered at Kom Ombo, and at Edfu there are famous wall carvings that depict the battle between Seth and Horus. His fame spread from the oases in the desert to the fertile land of the Delta, where he was worshipped at times. There are not many surviving statues of Seth, but the Egyptian Museum contains one of Seth and Horus crowning Ramesses III. Seth's figure in this piece was damaged, perhaps deliberately, but has now been restored.

## NEPHTHYS

Even though Nephthys was frequently mentioned in the ancient writings, she does not seem to have been the direct subject of worship, nor was she accorded her own cult center. The result is that, despite many references to her, not much can be determined about her, and myths in which she figures independently of Isis are almost non-existent.

Plate 17. Nephthys

She was the youngest of Nut's children and the sister and wife of Seth, but she does not seem to have suffered the repudiation accorded to her husband after his split with his family. On the contrary she sided with Isis in the family feud and repudiated her husband brother.

Since she was most often portrayed in consort with her older sister, she invites comparison with Isis, a comparison that reinforces the idea that Egyptians saw the world in terms of a duality. As Osiris and Seth represented sides of the duality, their sisters also represented opposites, even though they were viewed as companions rather than enemies. Nephthys assumed some of the characteristics of her husband, and while Isis represented life and birth, Nephthys represented death and decay. Isis stood for the visible, while her sister stood for the invisible. Isis was associated with light and day, whereas Nephthys was associated with darkness and night. The females of the Ennead should be seen as complementary. It is as if the Egyptians were suggesting that both sides of the duality must be considered at the same time.

Most of the duties accepted by Nephthys were shared with her sister. The Pyramid Texts explained that she had assisted Isis in collecting the parts of Osiris' body after Seth dismembered it and threw its parts into the Nile. One early scholar believed that both Isis and Nephthys were fertility counterparts of the god Min and that Nephthys' role was to assist in the resurrection of Osiris, an act that associated her with the concept of rebirth. In the Book of the Dead she was often depicted standing behind Osiris alongside Isis. Other vignettes showed her kneeling in adoration beside the sun disk as it was being raised into the sky. And still others showed her kneeling beside the bier of Osiris, assisting him to rise from the dead. She was also assigned the duty of protecting the organs of the dead. She, along with Isis, Neith, and Selket, was appointed guardian of the canopic jars which contained the organs of the dead person, and of the coffin containing the rest of his body. These are the four who can be observed spreading their arms in protection over King Tutankhamun's funeral chests at the Egyptian Museum.

Normally Nephthys was shown as a woman wearing a headdress surmounted by the hieroglyphic sign for her name. Literally the sign meant "Lady of the House." The sign had a rectangular shape, something like an altar, with a disk-like object over it. Manfred

Lurker thinks this was a wickerwork basket, which would be suitable for a goddess of the house. Others have thought it might represent a dish of water.

There is one interesting myth in which Nephthys plays a central part. According to this, Nephthys and Osiris were lovers, a fact which was discovered by Seth when Osiris left behind a garland which had fallen from his head during their lovemaking. There is even speculation that Anubis was born of this affair and was not Seth's child at all.

Even though Nephthys was not worshipped, she did play an important role in the worship of Osiris. There was a ritual at Abydos during the winter, in which two virgin priestesses paid homage to the god of the underworld. Two men dressed like Isis and Nephthys shaved their hair, wore lambswool wigs, and beat on tambourines while they chanted hymns to the god.

Today's visitor to Egypt can find numerous representations of Nephthys, but usually they are seen in conjunction with those of Isis. The Egyptian Museum contains several fine illustrations of Nephthys, especially those in the Tutankhamun exhibit. Down at Luxor Isis and her sister can be seen in such tombs as those of Seti I and Ramesses III where they are featured in wall paintings and carvings. At the beautiful small museum in Luxor Nephthys can be found on the mummy cartonnage (wrapping) of Shepenkhonsu.

# 3

# The Adventures of Ra

Since Ra, in his various forms and unions with other gods, was the sun god and father of the great Ennead, his adventures affected the entire universe. His power and brillance were great, his actions affected other gods and mortals alike. He had created the world and the gods and people who populated it, and he maintained his position of eminence as father of the gods even after others gained equal or greater power. As sun god, his chief function was to travel the skies daily and provide light and heat for the residents of earth; as chief god he was sometimes involved with other gods in events that were closely watched by all who might be influenced.

## The Daily Voyage of Ra Through the Sky

Understanding that the sun was fire, the early Egyptians could not easily conceive of it rising out of water without having been extinguished, yet it obviously came out of the water every day. They therefore pictured the sun as rising from the waters of Nun in a boat that could float and then sail through the air during the day. This daily victory over darkness caused men and women to live, nations to rejoice, and the souls of the dead to sing in joy. With good luck the boat had good winds and safe ports during its voyage. A hymn in the Book of the Dead celebrated Ra's daily glory: "Millions of years have

Plate 18. The solar boat with Ra in the center. He is served by Thoth and Maat, and
a falcon god who is fighting with Apophis.

gone over the world; I cannot tell the numbers of those through which you have passed. Your heart has decreed a day of happiness in the name of 'Traveller.' You pass over and travel through untold spaces [requiring] millions and hundreds of thousands of years [to pass over]; you pass through them in peace, and you steer your way through the watery abyss to the place you love; this you do in one little moment of time, and then you sink down and make an end of the hours.''

Actually there were two boats: Matet (which meant ''becoming stronger'') for the morning, and Semket (which meant ''becoming weak'') for the evening. Khepri, Ra and Atum, the various forms of the sun god during this journey, sat in the middle of the boat while Horus was the steersman at the rudder. Thoth, the god of wisdom, and Maat, the goddess of truth and justice, wrote down the daily course for the boat and then stood beside Horus to approve the course he set. Abtu and Ant were mythological fish that led the boats through the expanses of ocean. The king at his death joined the crew as Ra's immortal secretary. The king rode in the bow of the ship, where he opened Ra's boxes, broke open the sealed edicts, sealed his dispatches, sent out his messages, and generally did what Ra asked of him. He was also responsible for watching over Ra's jar of cold water during the day. The goddess Nehebka rode in the Matet boat; since she was the goddess of ''matter revivified,'' her presence caused considerable rejoicing among the dead souls who accompanied the ships during their voyages.

The boat settled into Manu, the mountains of the sunset, where as the evening boat it entered the waters of the underworld, called Tuat. As the sun set Horus, Hapi, Isis and Nephthys were seen in adoration. As if the nightly journey out of sight were not difficult enough, the boat was attacked during the night by its enemies. Although Ra carried with him a company of strong, wise and fair gods, of whom he was the strongest, his enemies never hesitated to try to find a weakness and destroy him. Collectively the enemies were Sebau, a legion of devils, but the most dangerous was Apophis (variant spelling: Apep) who took the form of a serpent. His attack on the sun god was seen as an attack on the stability of the world, and therefore his defeat was essential. Originally Apophis had been viewed as the darkness that surrounded Nun, and the first serious obstacle to the creation that Ra had to overcome. Later, however, Apophis personified the darkest part of the night which Ra must defeat before he could rise again in the morning. He attacked with mists, eclipses, and other phenomena that hide the light of the sun or moon. Ra counter-attacked with the darts of his sunbeams and sent his scorpions to sting the snake, but at the moment of greatest danger he left the boat and took the shape of a cat, an animal admired for its agility. In this form he cut off the head of the serpent. The nightly fate of Apophis was ghastly: he was bound in chains, then stabbed with spears, cut and dismembered with red-hot knives, and finally roasted and consumed by fire. Apophis was crafty and had many names to confuse Ra and his assistants, but the papyri listed them all so that the dead souls could help Ra to identify his enemy by the use of magic. The pink glow in the sky at evening was attributed to the blood that flowed from the wounded and defeated Apophis.

In the morning Ra arose again safe from the battles of the night, glorying in his victories over the powers of darkness. His brilliance undiminished, he sailed through the heavens on yet another of his daily voyages. His renewed presence gave new hope to those who depended on his light and warmth and was the cause of much rejoicing.

## The Sun God and the Phoenix

Sacred at Heliopolis, the phoenix was a mythological bird based on the wingtail or the heron. It was specially attached to Ra because it seemed to mimic the sun rising from the water when it took flight. Its Egyptian name (for "phoenix" is Greek) was bennu, which was derived from a word meaning "to shine" or "to rise." It was depicted with a long straight beak, graceful body, long legs, and two lengthy feathers falling from the back of its head. In the Coffin Texts the dead person viewed himself as rising like the phoenix: "I am that great phoenix which is in On, the supervisor of all that exists."

Elsewhere the texts associated the bird with Osiris or Horus since these gods and the bird existed for eternity. In the Book of the Dead there was a spell for helping the dead become the bennu bird: "I flew up as the Primeval God and assumed forms.... I am Horus, the god who gives light by means of his body."

The most elaborate discussion of the phoenix, however, came in Herodotus, who had some strange ideas that have become the conventional concept of the bird, even though they do not seem supported by Egyptian texts:

> They have also another sacred bird, which, except in a picture, I have never seen; it is called the phoenix. It is very uncommon, even among themselves; for according to the Heliopolitans, it comes there but once in the course of five hundred years, and then only at the decease of the parent bird. If it bear any resemblance to its picture, the wings are partly of a gold and partly of a crimson colour, and its form and size are perfectly like the eagle. They relate one thing of it that surpasses all credibility; they say that it comes from Arabia to the temple of the sun, bearing the dead body of its parent, enclosed in myrrh, which it buries. It makes a ball of myrrh, shaped like an egg, as large as it is able to carry, which it proves by experiment. This done it excavates the mass, into which it introduces the body of the dead bird; it again closes the aperture with myrrh, and the whole becomes the same weight as when composed entirely of myrrh; it then proceeds to Egypt to the temple of the sun.

These and other classical myths concerning the bird appear to be misreadings of the Egyptian concept. In Egypt the bird did not achieve immortality through periodic renewal, but it was seen as a symbol for the sun which did rise—like the bird—each day from the waters to the east. Perhaps the clearest Egyptian use of the bird was in the Book of the Dead where, as a sign of rebirth, it was beautifully depicted in the vignettes.

### Ra as Royal Father

In *Cult of the Sun*, her fine book on the sun god, Rosalie David has recorded a story of Ra's fathering of heirs to the earthly throne. The lengths to which kings of the fifth dynasty went to associate themselves with Ra, which included taking his name as part of their own, are suggestive of his power. These kings replaced the family of Cheops on the throne and used the Ra myth to justify their right to rule.

Plate 19. The phoenix

According to the myth, a magician by the name of Dedi was said to know the secret of the locks used by Thoth to keep his sanctuary inviolate; and Cheops, the builder of the greatest of the pyramids, sought this knowledge in order to secure his own structure. He sent for Dedi and asked for the secret, but the magician confessed that he did not in fact have it. He knew that the numbers which would open the locks of Thoth were kept in a flint casket in Heliopolis, but said that he was unable to open the chest and bring the numbers to the king. Instead, he promised, the secret would be brought to Cheops by the eldest son of Red-dedet. Since the king had never heard of such a woman and was puzzled by this prophecy, Dedi revealed that she was the wife of a priest of Ra and had conceived three children by the god himself. Ra had told her that her sons would be granted high power and would rule much of the land. Cheops grew sad at this news since he feared that his own children would be replaced by these sons of Ra, but Dedi, sensing his mood, assured him that Cheops' own son and grandson would rule before the children of Ra and Red-dedet. The king rewarded the old magician for this prophecy by making him a retainer in the royal household for the rest of his life.

When the time came for Red-dedet to deliver, Ra sent several of his deities to be present at the birth. Isis and Nephthys led the group and were assisted by Meshkhent (goddess of birth), Heket, and Khnum. The goddesses served as midwives and commanded the first-born to come from the womb without delay. Isis took the child from his mother's body and he came into this world with a head-cloth of lapis-lazuli and limbs adorned with gold. While the goddesses cut his umbilical cord and gave him his first bath, Meshkhent foretold that some day he would rule the land; Khnum, who formed babies' bodies on his potter's wheel, gave him health. Then each of his brothers was born, and the divinities performed the same services for them. Before leaving the children to the care of their mortal mother, the goddesses gave to the boys their royal crowns which were hidden in a locked room until they had need of them.

*****

This myth served a genuine political purpose. Cheops was succeeded by his son and grandson, and two more heirs beyond them;

but then the line of the fourth dynasty was broken and a new dynasty began. The eldest child mentioned in the myth became King Userkaf, a name supposedly given him at birth by Isis; and he and his brothers who also ruled in the fifth dynasty referred to themselves as "The Sons of Ra." This tale served to prove that the rulers of the fifth dynasty had divine authority for taking the throne. The two minor heirs of the builders of the pyramids of Giza were not mentioned in the myth, possibly because later generations were not likely to recognize their names or to consider them especially important. The myth did establish the significance of the cult of the sun god and demonstrated Ra's prestige.

## Ra in His Declining Years

In many ways Ra was the personification of numerous human needs recognized by early man, among which was the luxury of growing old and retiring from the day-to-day cares of the active world. Like a farmer who has grown too old to spend his entire day in the fields, Ra tired of the daily routine of rising in the east and setting in the west, always besieged by enemies. He looked forward to turning things over to his children, but like many mortals he was slow to recognize that the time of retirement was approaching, and had to be urged toward it by those around him. Some of the most interesting of his myths are set during this period of his life.

In one story, Ra complained of fatigue to Nun, the primeval waters, who set about trying to find him some help with his daily chores. First the sky-goddess Nut was instructed to take the form of a cow and carry Ra through the sky each day (a variation of this story said that Nut gave Ra the ride to help him escape from the angry survivors of mankind who did not take kindly to Hathor's destruction of so many of their friends and kin—see Chapter 7). Anyway, Nut became responsible for carrying Ra each day, but the strain was too much for her and her limbs began to tremble. Ra declared that he would find help for her and commanded her father Shu to support her belly (this is a variation of the myth that says Shu holds Nut up as the sky to separate her from the earth). When the men of earth saw Ra upon Nut's back, they began to regret their neglect of him. The next morning they appeared fully armed and ready to do battle against his enemies. Encouraged by their support, Ra immediately forgave mankind's earlier sins, which he attributed to the wiles of the earth's serpent population. Geb, as earth-god, was held responsible for the trouble caused by these malign creatures, and was ordered to take the necessary steps to see that the problems did not occur again.

Finally Ra called Thoth to come with haste into the chief god's court. Thoth was told, from that moment on, to keep a written record of the punishments Ra had decided for his enemies. Thoth was also to assume the title of Asti, Ra's deputy, and was to become Ra's representative on earth. In order to ease Thoth's task Ra created the ibis to be Thoth's messenger among men, gave him the use of the power of the sun and moon, and lastly—if this part of the inscription is properly understood—brought into being the ape to assist Thoth in driving back his enemies. Thus did Ra spread out the responsibilities of his divine office and make his life a little less wearisome.

This story was told on the walls of the tomb of Seti I near Luxor dating from the early part of the nineteenth dynasty (1320-1200 B.C.). The inscriptions are partly damaged, but most of the myth can be discovered and the rest guessed at. Nearby is a beautiful drawing of Nut as the cow goddess giving Ra a ride in his solar boats, but the exact connection between the drawing and the story remains the subject of considerable scholarly speculation.

## The Secret Name of Ra

Isis, observing the power and might of Ra, envied his control over all creatures. She knew that his power, like the breezes, reached to the far corners of the earth and the outmost expanses of the heavens, where he was revered by men and gods. In her heart she coveted this power and plotted to discover its secret so that she would be greater than the other gods and would rule over men. She was well-practiced in magic and sought a way of using this art to usurp her grandfather's supreme authority.

His power, however, lay in the fact that he alone knew his secret name. Every man and god had many names, but each kept the most potent of them to himself in order that others might not gain

Plate 20. Nut as the Cow. Ra can be seen in his boat by her front legs and Shu is supporting her belly.

dominion over him through its use. Ra's secret name was therefore his most carefully guarded possession. He knew that anyone who discovered the name could use it to gain his power over the world and even to obtain some control over Ra himself.

Many times he had risen in the morning and made his daily trip through the sky, only to see his radiance sink into the darkness of Tuat every night. The repetition of this act had tired him and he had grown so old and feeble that the saliva dribbled from his mouth and fell upon the earth. Seeing this, Isis quickly took up some of the ground mixed with the spittle and began to mold this clay into the shape of a cobra, the snake associated with the gods and kings of Egypt. The model snake contained Ra's own substance, therefore he had no defence against its poison.

Isis hid the serpent on the path Ra took each day on his heavenly journey; and next morning when Ra and his followers began their trip, the chief god passed close by the stealthy creature. The snake struck with all its divine force and sank its dart-like fangs into the flesh of the father of all the gods. The poison surged through Ra's body and caused great pain since it had been created from divine substance.

The cry of rage and pain that escaped from Ra shook heaven and earth; his followers in the boat gathered round to ask what had caused it. The pain was so great, however, that he could barely answer them. The poison spread through his body as the waters of the Nile spread over the land; his limbs trembled and his teeth chattered. Finally he calmed down enough to tell the gods in the boat that he had been seriously wounded. He was perplexed by the pain because he had thought himself safe from such an attack as long as he kept his name secret. He told them that he had just come out to take a look at the world he had created when something struck him and brought this intense pain, making him burn and shiver at the same time. Then he ordered that his children, the rest of the gods with knowledge of magic, be brought to consult with him.

With weeping and lamentations the gods assembled, but none could relieve the pain since it was caused by Ra's own substance. None had enough power to find a magical antidote. Naturally Isis was among those in the crowd, but she said nothing until the others had tried and failed to find a remedy. Calmly she practiced her deceit on the elderly god: "What is this, O divine Father? What is this? Has a snake brought pain to you? Has a creation of your hand lifted up its hand against you?'' She told him that she would use her magic on his behalf and find a cure.

Still confused by the severe pain, Ra described the symptoms to her: ''I am colder than water, I am hotter than fire. I tremble in all my limbs, and the sweat runs down my face even as in the heat of summer.'' This time Isis spoke quietly and softly and offered to help if he would reveal his secret name so that she could use it in her magic: ''Tell me your name, O divine Father, your true name, your secret name, for only he can live who is called by his name.''

Even in pain Ra recognized a trick, and his answer was a devious attempt to give her his names without revealing the ultimate secret: ''I am the maker of heaven and earth, I am the establisher of the mountains, I am the creator of the waters, I am the maker of the secrets of the two horizons. I am light and I am darkness, I am the maker of the hours, the creator of days. I am the opener of festivals, I am the maker of running streams, I am the creator of living flame. I am Khepri in the morning, Ra at noontime, and Atum in the evening.''

Isis heard all the words but knew that he had not given her what she wanted. She remained quiet and let the poison work a little more on his old body. She realized that he had not revealed the secret name; the names he had given her were known to many men and gods alike. This information could hardly increase her power. When the pain became more intense, she finally spoke: ''Your name, your true name, your secret name, was not among those. Tell me your name in order that the poison may be driven out of your body, for only he whose name I know can be healed by my magic.''

At this moment the pain grew worse and Ra realized that the time had come to give up something of himself in order to find peace. He took Isis aside where the others would not hear and the two began to bargain like merchants in a bazaar, but Ra was in too much pain to bargain well. Isis demanded that he take an oath to give Horus, her son, his two eyes—the sun and moon. He agreed and whispered the secret name. She was faithful to her bargain and issued the proper curse to relieve the pain: ''Depart, poison, go forth from Ra. O Eye of Horus, go forth from the god and shine outside his mouth. It is I who work, it is I who make the vanquished poison fall down upon the

69

earth, for the name of the great god has been taken from him. Let Ra live, and let the poison die! Let the poison die, and let Ra live!" She, of course, never revealed the secret name since she had no desire to share her new-found power with anyone else, and so this special name remains hidden from all mortals and gods to this day. Isis finally did not use the power for her own sake, but to increase the power of her son. Horus replaced his great great-grandfather as the sun god once he had the eyes for his own use. The Eye of Ra became the Eye of Horus and the elderly god was given a graceful retirement in which he was revered as the creator of all things but did not have daily responsibilities. Horus was now to be considered the chief god.

*****

Among many early societies it was thought that the real name of a person or god was essential to their existence. This name was the key to their being, for without a name nothing exists. To know the name was to have power over the creature, and the myth of Ra and Isis was told to illustrate the importance of keeping one's true name secret, or at least reserved for special occasions. In accordance with this belief, ancient Egyptian kings always had several names. One of them would probably be compounded with the name of a god and would be used only in a religious context or on monuments. The cartouches of the kings, therefore, may reveal several names, one being reserved for religious purposes. In connexion with this myth, too, we may note that the Egyptians did not think of their gods as creatures who freely gave of themselves to the human beings for whom they were responsible. Their gifts —eternal life, for instance—had to be exacted by force, and it was therefore necessary for mortals to gain some sort of power over the gods in order to obtain unusual blessings. One way to this power was the secret name.

This myth has survived in two papyri, one at Turin and the other in the British Museum. The one at Turin, which has been translated by M.A. Murray and E.A. Wallis Budge, dates from the twentieth dynasty (about 1200 to 1085 B.C.). The version given here was based on Murray's, but it has been modernized and references to Budge's version have been used to expand it. This tale was originally told to illustrate the value of curses against serpents, and the text presents magic formulae to cure snake bites. The magician was probably supposed to recite the tale in the hope that the words of magic which could cure a god would have the same effect on the human patient. The original text tells us that these magical spells were to be spoken over images of Atum, Horus, and Isis in order to cure the stricken man of the serpent's poison.

# 4

# The Adventures of Osiris and Isis

The myths concerning Osiris and his sister-wife are among the most entertaining and illuminating of Egyptian mythology. The story of Osiris' murder and Isis' hunt for his body is known worldwide and is an integral statement of Egyptian beliefs in life after death. R.T. Rundle Clark calls Osiris "the most vivid achievement of the Egyptian imagination."

Actually no complete Egyptian version of the stories has survived from ancient times, and the earliest version was written down by Plutarch, the Greek traveler and historian from the first century after Christ. For the next four hundred years, other Western writers such as Diodorus Siculus, Firmicus Maternus, and Macrobius recounted the adventures of the two gods and added details of their own to the stories. Much of this non-Egyptian material has been confirmed as authentic by Egyptologists working in temples and other sites where murals tell fragmented stories of the divine pair. Finally, the Pyramid Texts and other early writings contain numerous references to Osiris and Isis and help complete the story when pieced together. What is told here is a compilation of these sources, but Plutarch's writings provide the basic outline.

## The Murder of Osiris and Isis' Hunt for His Body

Osiris was first a legendary leader of men while in human form. At the moment of his birth a voice announced: "The lord of all the world

72

is born." Other supernatural signs pointed to the occurrence of a marvelous event, especially at a temple at Thebes where a man named Pamyles had gone to draw a jug of water. He heard a voice commanding him to go forth among the people proclaiming that "the good and great King Osiris was then born." Having fulfilled his charge, Pamyles was rewarded by the grateful gods by being given the responsibility for Osiris' education.

Osiris was born a god but grew up as a man. He became king of Egypt at a time when the country was full of wild men who knew only the habits of barbarism (including cannibalism, according to some versions of the myth). As a civilizing force for these people, Osiris discovered methods of organized agriculture and taught his people how to cultivate corn and barley. He was the first man to drink wine and showed his people how to plant vines to provide grapes for this remarkable new beverage. In order to refine their rough customs, Osiris instructed the citizens of his land in rituals for honoring the gods, and gave them laws to govern their behavior. He relied heavily on the advice of Thoth who taught men rhetoric and names for objects which heretofore had been nameless. Thoth invented the letters of the alphabet, arithmetic, music, sculpture, and astronomy—gifts which Osiris passed on to the humans for their betterment. The people recognized that Osiris was responsible for improving their lives and greatly revered his ideas.

Satisfied with his progress at home, Osiris decided to export his civilization to other lands. First he arranged for Isis to govern Egypt while he was gone and gave her Thoth as assistant. Then he marched toward Ethiopia with an army and a few friends. Greeted by a company of satyrs for his entertainment, he added musicians and dancers to their numbers. He taught the local inhabitants agricultural methods, constructed dams and canals to control the flooding of the Nile, and built cities. In areas too dry to grow grapes, he taught the people to make beer from barley. He then passed through Arabia on his way to India, where he built cities and introduced the ivy plant. Next he traveled across the Hellespont into Europe where he was forced to kill a king who resisted his new and fair system of government.

During his absence Isis had no serious problems since she was careful and cautious; but Seth, their brother, was jealous of Osiris' success, his land, and his wife. He bided his time and plotted the assassination of the king. He gathered around him seventy-two conspirators and convinced Aso, a queen of Ethiopia who presumably was jealous of Osiris' success in her country, to join the plot. The hypocritical conspirators greeted their king with smiles when he returned home, but in their hearts they were plotting murder. Seth, who had secretly taken the measurements of Osiris' body, constructed a fine chest to fit those measurements exactly. This richly decorated wooden box was a prize worthy of any man or god. At a feast at Seth's banquet hall, the guests drank wine and sang songs while slaves scattered flowers about the room. At the height of the entertainment, the chest was borne in while the guests cried out in appreciation of its beauty. With words sweet as honey, Seth told those gathered there: "He who lies down in this coffin and whom it fits, to that man I will give it." The guests eagerly stepped forward, but each found that it was not the right size. When all the others had failed to fit the chest, Seth jokingly challenged the king to try. Proudly Osiris stepped into the chest and lay down to discover that it was a perfect fit, but no sooner was he inside than the conspirators slammed the lid over his head. While some nailed the top tight, others poured hot lead around the edge so that Osiris quickly suffocated. The party guests then took the chest to the Nile and threw it with its divine contents into the waters, which carried them far away.

At that time Isis was visiting the village of Chemmis not far from Thebes in Upper Egypt. The fauns and satyrs in that area were the first to know of their king's assassination, and they quickly spread word of the horror. Isis, however, knew immediately of her husband's death without having to be told and went into mourning. She cut off a lock of hair and put on mourning robes without moving from the spot on which she stood. Ever since, the town has been known as Koptos, or the City of Mourning.

Full of grief, Isis set out looking for the chest and its contents. She wandered across the country and inquired of everyone she met whether he had news of her husband's body. Nowhere did she receive help until she chanced across some children playing near her road. They told her they had indeed seen the chest being thrown into the river and floating northward toward the sea. From this time on, Egyptians revered children for their prophetic powers.

74

During her mourning Isis was told that her sister Nephthys had fallen in love with Osiris and tricked him into her bed. A garland he had left behind after the event was proof of the truth of the story. Rumor said that Nephthys had become pregnant from the occasion, but fearing the reaction of her husband Seth, she had left the baby boy to be exposed immediately after his birth. Wild dogs found the child and saved him, and Isis soon located the pack and rescued her nephew. She took the young god to be reared as her own son and gave him the name of Anubis. From this time onward he watched over Isis the way mortal dogs watch over humans. Isis was quick to forgive Nephthys, and the two females shared their grief for Osiris. Even though Nephthys was married to Seth, she soon left him and devoted herself to the search for Osiris' body. The songs of lamentation sung by the sisters were described by the scholar James Breasted as "the most sacred expression of sorrow known to the heart of the Egyptian."

Eventually Isis heard that the body had been washed ashore at a place called Byblos, but there is disagreement over just where this was. Some accept the Greek notion that it was on the coast of Syria; others believe that it was a corruption of the name for a papyrus swamp in the Delta of Egypt. Whichever it was, Isis went there in search of the chest. The waves had carried it ashore and lifted it into the branches of a tamarisk tree growing nearby. When the tree grew to encompass and hide the chest, its gigantic size and beautiful flowers made it widely known, and eventually King Malkander and his wife Queen Athenais came from the palace to see the marvelous sight. He ordered the tree to be cut down and used as a pillar to support the roof of his palace, but no one suspected that this piece of wood contained the body of a king and god.

Following the information from the children, Isis traced the passage of the chest to Byblos where she came ashore and sat without speaking. The queen's handmaidens, coming to bathe in the waters, were struck by the sight of this beautiful woman who sat so quietly. Fascinated, they began a conversation with the stranger who was dressed in white with her breast exposed after the fashion of the Egyptians. She showed them how to braid their hair and wear their jewels, and her breath perfumed the women and their clothes with a wonderful fragrance. On their return to the palace the queen inquired about the fragrance, and they told her of the beautiful stranger. When she went to the shore, the two women immediately became companions and Isis was invited to attend Athenais at court.

The infant son of the queen suffered from an incurable illness, but Isis offered to restore him to health: "I can make him strong and well, but in my own way I will do it, and no one must interfere." Every day the child seemed stronger, but no one knew what Isis did to help him. Finally the queen hid herself in the nursery to uncover Isis' secret, and what she saw shocked her. Isis first locked the doors and then built a high scorching flame behind them. Putting the child to the flames, she turned herself into a swallow which flew around and around the pillar making the most mournful twitterings. The queen in fright seized her son and began to run from the room but suddenly she was confronted, not by a strange woman, but by Isis the goddess. "O foolish mother," said the goddess, "Why did you seize the child? But a few days longer and all that is mortal in him would have been burned away and he would have been like the gods—immortal and forever young." The mother regretted her haste but recognized that she was in the presence of divinity. When she and her husband asked the goddess to accept a gift for restoring their son to health, all Isis asked for was the pillar supporting the roof. As soon as this unusual request was granted, she sent for carpenters who split open the trunk and removed the chest. Isis then had the men bind the tree back together and wrap it in fine linens. She strewed it with spices and scented flowers and returned it to the king and queen. (This became the djed pillar which was worshipped from that day on by the people of Byblos because it had once held the remains of Osiris. Its use spread throughout Egypt where it became a symbol of strength.) This done, Isis flung herself on the chest and began her lament for her husband. The sight of the goddess in such distress was so terrible that one of the king's sons died of fright.

Isis loaded the chest and body on a ship and set sail for home with the elder of the king's sons as a passenger. During the voyage she opened the chest and fell in grief over the body. The boy had crept up silently behind her and, when she heard him, she looked round with such terror that he too died on the spot. So it was that the king and queen of Byblos lost a second son to the lamentations of the goddess.

Plate 21. Djed pillar holding an ankh and the rising sun

During the voyage Osiris' body rested on the open deck. When the waves and currents from a little river they were passing caused the ship to rock, Isis used her magic to dry up the waters.

Once she had arrived in the safety of the Delta, she set the chest on land and she and Nephthys tried to revive Osiris. A beautiful hymn extolled Isis' efforts to love her husband as before; she is said to be the goddess:

Who worked on your lifeless body with knotted cords,
Who warmed your body with the warmth of her breast,
Who made air to enter with the beating of her wings,
Who made life flow from your body up into Isis,
To the chamber of the abode of life.

The hymn explains that her magic was able to warm and breathe life into Osiris' body long enough for it to stir and impregnate her with Horus. The walls of the Temple of Dendera depict graphically the awakening of Osiris and Isis' appearance as a bird hovering over her husband's erect penis from which she received the seed that enabled her to continue the great line of the gods.

Seth hunted Isis down and shut her into a dark prison, but with the help of Anubis, she escaped and fled into the swamps. When the time came for her to deliver her child, she sat alone among the reeds of the river. Her pain was great, but no matter how hard she strained, no matter how hard she pushed, the baby would not be born. Suddenly two gods appeared at her side and smeared her forehead with blood—a sign of life—and finally her body split and the boy sprang forth, like the sun when it breaks from darkness. As the day of his birth was the vernal equinox, the beginning of spring, Horus appeared at the time young shoots of grain were beginning to sprout from the darkness of the ground.

Once Horus was born, Thoth appeared to his mother and urged her to flee with the child to protect him from his evil, red-haired uncle. The great god of wisdom advised her to hide the little boy until he was old enough to "assume the office of Ruler of the Two Lands." His mother then took Horus deep into the swamps of Lower Egypt where she placed her baby under the care of the goddess Uazet who resided at Pe, a city on a floating island. Isis loosened the ropes

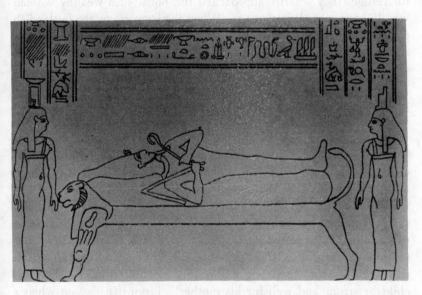

Plate 22. Isis with Osiris' body

that held the island fast and allowed it to drift further into the swamp where no man or god would know where to locate it or its divine resident.

During the time of her flight with Horus, much adversity befell the goddess who felt utterly alone against the world while she walked far with her baby and her seven scorpion companions. Once, looking for refuge, they wearily approached the house of a wealthy woman who lived in a small settlement. When the woman saw the outlandish party, she hurriedly shut her door against them, not knowing whom she was turning away. Chagrined and hurt, Isis continued her wanderings. After a time she found rest in the home of another woman, but her anger with the first continued unabated. Six of her scorpions transfered all their poison into the sting of one, Tefen, who slipped through a crack under the woman's door and stung her son with the power of seven scorpions. Despite his mother's piteous lamentations, the child soon died. The woman rushed about the town trying to find help, but this time it was she who was denied admission to other houses. In the midst of her grief she remembered her treatment of the strange woman who so much needed a friend, and she repented of her behavior now that she understood what it meant to be alone and rejected. Isis then showed mercy, calling upon her scorpions to withdraw their poison: "The child shall live, the poison shall die! As Horus is strong and well for me, his mother, so shall this child be strong and well for his mother!" From that day on when a mortal suffered the sting of the scorpion, these words of Isis were used as a charm to relieve the effects of the poison.

Later, Isis left her home in the swamp disguised as a beggar woman, for the great goddess had been reduced to begging for food to keep her son alive. When she returned home, she discovered the boy lying on the ground with tears in his eyes and saliva flowing from his mouth. Not even milk from a divine breast could ease his pain, and never had Isis felt more desperate. Finally there appeared a woman bearing an ankh, who diagnosed the source of the problem: a scorpion bite. Isis repeated a series of charms, but nothing relieved the child's pain. Then again Thoth appeared to the mother. He had just come, he said, from the solar boat where the gods were worried. The sun was standing still and the world would remain in darkness until the sun god of the future was cured. The anguished mother chided her

**Plate 23. Isis nursing Horus in the papyrus swamp, attended by Thoth and Amun-Ra**

old friend for moving so slowly. Didn't he understand how much Horus suffered? Thoth in his own time assured her that he had come to help and finally began to recite a long charm designed to kill the poison; soon his ministrations had the desired effect. Once the child began to recover, Thoth ordered the women of the Delta to help protect Horus from his enemy and assured them that one day he would rule the Two Lands with the help of Ra, Osiris, and Isis. The god of wisdom then returned to the solar boat to report to the boy's father that all was well below.

All was not well, however, for Osiris and Isis. Seth was not satisfied that he was safe as long as Osiris' body existed. After Isis and Nephthys had embalmed the body with the assistance of Anubis and Thoth who had been sent for this task by Ra, Isis hid the body and set out to visit Horus at Pe. While she was gone, Seth went hunting wild boars by moonlight: he enjoyed the evil things that roamed at night. He was at full gallop after a boar when he saw the finely-wrought chest he had used to trick Osiris, and reined in his horse. Gleefully he jerked the body from the chest and tore it into fourteen pieces. Some said that he then scattered the pieces across Egypt, but the more widely accepted myth is that he threw the pieces into the Nile and let the waters carry them the length of the river. Then he laughed aloud and boasted across the world: "It is not possible to destroy the body of a god, but I have done what is impossible, I have destroyed Osiris." But Seth was mistaken.

Isis once more set out on a search for her husband's body, but this time she had to find its parts. Attended by birds and beasts, she sailed up and down the Nile in a frail boat of papyrus reeds lashed together. The dreaded crocodile avoided the boat and refused to harm its divine passenger, thus originating the belief that the crocodile will not attack anybody floating in a papyrus boat. One by one Isis found the dismembered parts of Osiris. Wherever she found one, she pretended to bury it and to build a shrine marking the spot. Actually, according to Diodorus, Isis made a waxen mold of each part, presented it to local priests and swore them to protect forever this "part" of the god's body. In return she promised each priest the personal use of one third of the land set aside for the worship of Osiris. The historian explained the results: "Accordingly it is said that the priests, mindful of the benefits of Osiris, desirous of gratifying the queen, and moved by the prospect of gain, carried out all the instructions of Isis." While some believed that she actually buried the god's parts in these shrines and tombs, most accepted the idea that this was part of an elaborate ruse to trick Seth, and that she took the real parts of Osiris' body to Horus in order that he might put them together again. It seems that she found all but one of the parts: the god's sexual organ, which had been eaten by fish—the lepidotus, phagrus, and oxyrhynchus. Unable to reassemble the body completely, Isis made a mold of the missing part and, according to Plutarch, "instituted a solemn festival to its memory, which is even to this day observed by the Egyptians." Unfortunately for the curious, this festival seems not to have survived Plutarch's day.

Isis' trick of pretending to bury the body wherever she found a part helps to explain why there are so many shrines to Osiris. Each site jealously guarded its claim to have responsibility for protecting the god, and before many centuries had passed new sites arose claiming to be authentic too.

As Isis delivered the parts of Osiris' body, Horus—with the assistance of Anubis and Thoth—set about reassembling it. Once it was all together, except of course the part eaten by the fish, the body was wrapped in white linen and placed in state at the Temple of Abydos. After Horus had fought his battle with Seth, he returned to Abydos with the eye he had won from his evil uncle. Osiris sat on a throne with his arms crossed holding the flail and scepter. Horus reverently opened his father's mouth and allowed him to eat of the eye, which gave him eternal life (the mythic origin of the ritual of the Opening of the Mouth). Horus then put into place a long ladder that stretched from Abydos to heaven, and slowly Osiris climbed upward, accompanied by Isis and Nephthys wearing beautiful robes. Thoth followed carrying the book of the gods, and Horus helped his father climb whenever he needed slight assistance. As he climbed higher, Osiris was able to see the mountains to the east and west and feel the cool breezes from the four corners of the earth. The solar boat lighted his passage and finally he stepped out onto the crystal floor of heaven which rested on the peaks of two mountains. Now an immortal, it became his task to judge the lives of the mortals who sought to follow him.

Diodorus wrote that Isis, after she had seen to the survival of Osiris' body and the continuation of his worship, made a vow never to marry again. She remained the perfect queen to her people and was renowned for her sense of justice and her charity. Her efforts to revive both her son and husband from illness and death created in her an interest in medicine which she was later able to use to help mankind. At her death some claimed that she was buried at Memphis, while others believe she was put to rest in her temple at Philae. After death, she is supposed to have taken her place among the rest of the gods, especially in support of Osiris. Her fame in medicine was widespread.

The buildings erected in Osiris' memory gave Egypt some fine examples of religious architecture, but the most outstanding was the Temple at Abydos, which claimed to be the repository of his head. A stele describes in detail the festival in which Ikhernefert, an official during the twelfth dynasty, played the important role of Horus. This was a sort of play which began with a procession of priests, laymen, a representation of Horus, and a boat holding a statue of the god Osiris. Horus engaged the enemies of Osiris in battle when they attacked the boat, and many of the people defended the great god, but he was nevertheless slain. Probably (the text is not clear on this) Isis and Nephthys found the body and began the rituals of lamentation. Horus then directed that the body be buried at Peger, whose location has never been determined by later scholarship. Following the burial, Horus sought out Osiris' enemies and avenged his father's death in a great battle; the theatrical recreation of this event must have been one of the more thrilling and dangerous parts of the play. After his victory, Horus set Osiris in a boat to sail before the crowds of people gathered at Abydos to celebrate the defeat of Seth and his troops, and to greet the risen god. It is possible that the performance of the play and the following festivities could have lasted three or four weeks.

Memphis also claimed to have the buried head, and enough temples claimed possession of his legs to have more than adequately equipped him with several pairs.

The djed pillar, which entered the Osiris myth as the tree containing his coffin, was also connected with an important festival in his honour. Many of the symbols found in Egyptian mythology had foreign origins, but two—the eye and the djed pillar—were distinctly

Egyptian. Although the latter came to be associated with the god Osiris, it was probably a pre-historic Egyptian fetish. In shape, this object was a tallish pillar that flared out to provide a base when expected to stand alone; otherwise it had the same diameter from top to bottom and was planted in the ground like a maypole. Near the top were four cross-members which gave the appearance of short limbs or branches. The word djed meant "stability."

Manfred Lurker believes that the pillar was originally a symbolic fertility pole on which were tied ears of corn in tiers (hence the cross-members). The ritualistic use of the pillar began in Memphis, according to Lurker, where it was associated with Ptah, who was called the "noble djed" in the Old Kingdom. If so, the king probably helped to raise the pillar in order to associate his reign with stability. R.T. Rundle Clark finds a different origin: he points out that in the Old Kingdom the pillar was shown in wall decorations at the Step Pyramid at Sakkara. In these drawings djed pillars were shown in the royal palace where they formed columns supporting windows. When one looked through the windows, the pillars gave the appearance of holding up the sky beyond. Clark writes: "The purpose is clear:... the djed columns are world pillars, holding up the sky and so guaranteeing the space of air and world in which the king's authority holds good." Clark believes that in the pre-historic era the pillar was part of a "simple harvest ritual" performed by peasants in the Delta.

Both scholars agree that, whatever its physical origins, the djed pillar found a place in mythology once the Osiris myths were widely disseminated. In the Pyramid Texts the pillar was connected with Osiris and described as being charred. It was thought of as the tree which grew up around Osiris' coffin after the waters of the Nile had floated it away. Isis had used fire as part of the ritual of release, which would account for the references to charred wood. Reference was also made to the top lying beside the pillar, which makes sense if the top were the branches of the tree which had been cut off when the tree was felled to be used in the king's palace as a column.

At the Delta town of Busiris there was an annual festival in which Osiris's dismembered body was reconstituted. Here, apparently, the pillar came to stand for his backbone (which could also explain its shape), and in this festival it was erected as part of the ritual. Coffins in the New Kingdom had the pillar painted on the bottom as a suggestion that the corpse became Osiris when his backbone became one with the painted one. A wall painting at the Temple of Seti I at Abydos shows a series of scenes in which the king assisted Isis in raising the pillar and thereby resurrecting Osiris. The obvious phallic symbolism of the totem also suggested the sexual resurrection of Osiris, commemorated elsewhere at this temple. In other drawings of the pillar here and there throughout Egypt it is shown with arms holding the crook and flail in the same attitude often used for Osiris; and vignettes in the Book of the Dead, as well as drawings elsewhere, showed the pillar with eyes staring out between the cross-members, just as if Osiris were looking out from inside.

*****

The popularity of the Osiris-Isis myth has led many scholars to try to explain its significance. Most interpretations can probably be reduced to three simple themes: the transferral of the power of kingship, celebration of the cycle of nature and its annual rejuvenation, and rituals for achieving immortality.

Older scholars, such as E.A. Wallis Budge and James Frazer, were chiefly interested in the myth as a statement about death and resurrection. Budge, of course, wrote a massive study of Osiris and did not limit himself to any one aspect of the myth, but the motif of resurrection lies at the heart of all his research. Frazer compared Osiris to the Greek gods Adonis and Attis in one of the most important volumes of *The Golden Bough* and concluded: "In the resurrection of Osiris the Egyptians saw the pledge of a life everlasting for themselves beyond the grave. They believed that every man would live eternally in the other world if only his surviving friends did for his body what the gods had done for the body of Osiris. Hence the ceremonies observed by the Egyptians over the human dead were an exact copy of those which Anubis, Horus, and the rest had performed over the dead god."

Rudolf Anthes believes that the myth was a statement of the way ritual serves to satisfy religious needs, because the rituals associated with the resurrection of Osiris became an important part of Egyptian culture. Anthes notes the ludicrous elements in the story, especially in the Horus-Seth conflict (to be told in the next chapter); but he believes that the common people worshipped the gods and enjoyed

**Plate 24.** Osiris as judge. The children of Horus stand before him on the Lotus, while Isis and Nephthys support him from behind

the story-telling aspect of the tales at the same time. There was great dignity in the rituals associated with Osiris and Isis, and some of the hymns and charms that have survived are literary works of considerable beauty.

The myth of Osiris is intimately connected with the Egyptian view of death, according to Siegfried Morenz: "Egyptian religion, in so far as it was related to death, preserved ancient ways of ensuring everlasting life and kept on discovering new ones." Egyptian religion maintained the beliefs that life would be prolonged in the tomb and that the deceased man and the possessions in his tomb could be rejuvenated through certain rituals. The best way for a dead king to transcend death was "to become Osiris" through the clearly prescribed ritual which would unite the king with the god, thereby raising him above the possibility of being judged like other mortals. The myth of Osiris, then, provided a ritualistic method for overcoming death.

The best way to approach this myth, as R.T. Rundle Clark has written, is to seek its symbolic value. Out of the story emerges a man-god who is

> the essential victim. Yet he is avenged and his passion has an end at last, when justice and order are re-established on earth. The other gods are transcendent, distinct from their worshippers. Osiris, however, is immanent. He is the sufferer with all mortality but at the same time he is all the power of revival and fertility in the world. He is the power of growth in plants and of reproduction in animals and human beings. He is both dead and the source of all living. Hence to become Osiris is to become one with the cosmic cycles of death and rebirth.

The myth, then, is finally seen in archetypal terms.

# 5

# Horus

Of all the gods of Egyptian mythology the most complex and potentially confusing for us today is Horus. One Egyptologist from the turn of the century identified fifteen different forms of this god, and Siegfried Morenz also found fifteen, not necessarily the same ones. The main forms were probably Ra-Herakhty, Horus the Elder, Horus the Younger, and Horus the Child. Ra-Herakhty was a form of the sun god, a combination of Ra and Horus representing the morning sun. Often shown in falcon form or in the shape of the winged disk, he was worshipped from Heliopolis to Abu Simbel. Horus the Elder can be considered the fifth child of Geb and Nut, making him another brother of Isis and Osiris. Some have thought that he might be the son of Hathor, but in that case his paternity is in doubt, although Ra is sometimes mentioned. Horus the Younger should be considered the son of Isis and Osiris, the god who avenged his father's murder and replaced him on earth, the hero of the war with Seth to be told in the next chapter. Horus the Child was another version of Horus the Younger, but he was given distinct depiction. Called Harpocrates by the Greeks, he was prominent during the Graeco-Roman period, long after the other forms of Horus. Horus the Child was usually shown as a boy, wearing the side-lock of a youth and sticking his finger in his mouth. At the height of his popularity he was often commemorated on small bronze plaques, called the cippi of Horus, where he was

Plate 25. Horus as falcon wearing the crowns of Upper and Lower Egypt

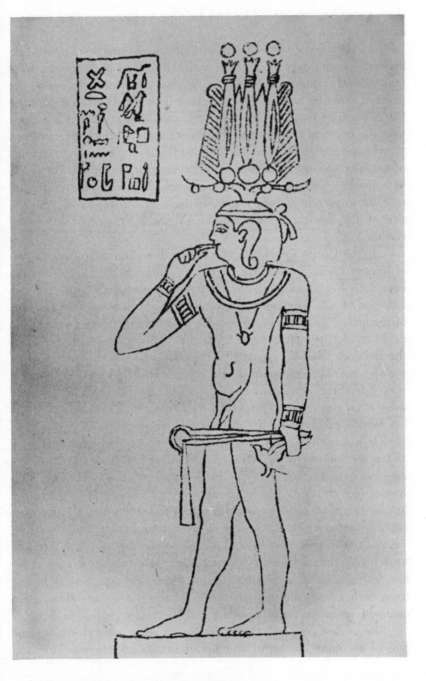

Plate 26.  Harpocrates

shown standing on crocodiles and holding scepters or other signs of authority.

At Edfu some of the forms of Horus came together. Following his early victory over the army of Seth, Horus and his followers came ashore near Edfu to celebrate. To commemorate the event, Ra decreed that the winged disk, the form Horus had taken during the battle when he fought as Ra-Herakhty, should be preserved as a motif over the doors of temples and shrines as a sign that the gods protected all who entered. Visitors can still find these images among the ruins of temples and other shrines. (Following this event Edfu became a base for the worship of Horus; centuries later during the Ptolemaic rule, an important temple was built there which was to become the site of the festival celebrating the sacred marriage of Horus and Hathor.)

In the Coffin Texts, this Horus was thought of mainly as the son of Isis and Osiris—whom we are calling Horus the Younger—and had been fully assimilated into the Heliopolitan genealogy as a character united with Ra. The victorious Horus thought of himself as the chief of the gods: "I am Horus, the Falcon who is on the battlements of the mansion of Him whose name is hidden. My flight aloft has reached the horizon, I have overpassed the gods of the sky, I have made my position more prominent than that of the Primeval Ones. .. My place is far from Seth, the enemy of my father Osiris. .. I go up in flight and there is no god who can do what I have done. .. I am Horus, born of Isis whose protection was made within the egg."

It was in the Coffin Texts that the images of Horus as the falcon and as the son of Isis merged, according to R.T. Rundle Clark. As we have seen in the myth of his birth, he was usually depicted as a human-like child in need of his mother Isis' nursing and protection; but in other versions he was born not as a child but as a falcon. During pregnancy Isis knew that her baby was unusual and told Atum "it is a falcon that is within my body." When the baby was born, he took flight while his mother immediately began to negotiate a seat for him in the solar boat. In this version Horus did not grow up hiding from Seth among the papyrus rushes of the Delta, but immediately assumed his place as a powerful god.

Regardless of which myth is followed, as an adult Horus became one of the most powerful and important gods. He was first and foremost a sun god, and the replacement of Osiris here on earth, with a place in the solar boat as its pilot and steersman.

Of all Egyptian mythological symbols the most enduring is the eye. Actually there were two eyes in the early myths—one associated with Ra and another with Horus. We have seen the myth in which Ra himself had two eyes, the sun and the moon. Since Horus was at times amalgamated with Ra, it is not surprising that Ra's second eye became the Eye of Horus. This eye became the particular object of Seth's aggression during the battle between Horus and his uncle; and when the red god, using his magical powers of deception, had captured the eye, he threw it into the darkness beyond the edge of the world. Thoth, who had been watching the fight and who was the guardian of the moon, observed where it fell and went to fetch it. When he found it, it was in pieces; but he located them all and put them together to form a full moon and thereby restored the night light. This eye was called the *wedjat* and ancient Egyptians could take the eye apart into its pieces. In fact, the various pieces were used in early writing to represent fractions (the eyeball, for example, represented one-quarter).

Other myths gave Horus duties as a creator, protector of kings, and agent of the dead in the underworld. It was the Book of the Gates, a lesser-known collection of instructions for dealing with the next life, that assigned Horus a role as creator, in particular, of the black race. According to this myth, the Egyptians were once the only race on earth. Then Horus and Sekhmet joined together to create those people who dwelled in the desert beyond the so called Black Land, obviously named for the rich soil along the Nile. The text is confusing in parts, but apparently Horus created the black race and Sekhmet created the fair-skinned Libyans. The two gods consequently became responsible for protecting the souls of their creations in the afterlife. According to Siegfried Morenz, Thoth then created the multiplicity of languages which was to separate the races. Thoth also seems to have acted as something of an interpreter when foreigners came to the gates of the underworld seeking eternal life, although it must have been Horus and Sekhmet who acted as their spokesmen during their trials.

The role of protector of kings was another assigned to Horus rather early in history. It was through association with Horus that the

Plate 27. The falcon as sun god

king gained his divinity, and the names of some early kings show that they were thought of as Horus while they reigned. This association gave them the power and authority of the gods while they were still alive. Since the king was believed to be Horus here on earth, an interesting problem arose: How could the immortal god Horus die when the king as Horus passed from mortal life? Everyone knew that a god could not die, yet every so often Horus, as the king, did just that. The answer to this theological problem was probably found in the Heliopolitan mythology into which Horus was assimilated. It came to be believed that while the king was alive, he was Horus; but when he died he immediately became Osiris and his successor became Horus in his turn.

Horus earned his reputation as protector of the dead through his efforts in behalf of his father in the underworld. It was Horus who received the parts of Osiris' body as they were recovered by Isis; and he, Anubis, and Thoth embalmed the body, reassembled the pieces, and wrapped them in mummy-cloth. Horus then originated the ceremony of the Opening of the Mouth when he fed his own eye to Osiris in order to assure eternal life for the slain god. In the Book of the Dead, Horus had substantial duties in the underworld, although his role never rivaled that of Anubis or Thoth, much less that of Osiris. Horus was the guide of the dead through the early stages of their trial, and was shown in vignettes leading the recently deceased person by the hand. He was involved sometimes in the Opening of the Mouth, and had the important duty of presenting the souls which passed the trial to Osiris for final acceptance.

*****

The myths of Horus can be variously interpreted. They share several themes common to other mythologies and folklores: the hiding of the infant, the young adult's search for his true father, the great battles. Horus is an early example of a hero typical of much epic poetry. But Horus transcends the heroic archetype. He was the savior of the world, who in restoring the vitality of the king brought renewal to the earth itself. He was the protagonist in the struggle between the forces of good and evil, and his victory assured the salvation of the earth and its inhabitants. His triumph over Seth placed evil "under his sandals," as the Coffin Texts put it.

95

Plate 28.  The eye

The worship of Horus was widespread, which is not surprising given the numerous forms in which he could be found. At Abu Simbel, over the entrance to the Temple of Ramesses II, there is a falcon representing the sun god with the baboons of Thoth in respectful attendance. At Luxor many of the tombs contain murals of Horus, usually in human shape with a hawk's head. In the Egyptian Museum in Cairo there is a large number of statues of Horus, most often in falcon form. The chief cult center for Horus was, of course, Edfu; and the temple there, begun by Ptolemy II, is the most perfectly preserved of all Egyptian temples. The black granite statue of Horus at the entrance is one of Egypt's most valuable works of art.

# 6

# Horus' Battle with Seth

Horus' attempts to avenge his father's murder and to regain control over the territory taken by Seth led to the great battles of Egyptian mythology.  The tale begins with a young son who seeks to avenge his father's death; but it leads on to become a fight for the territory or position that the son thinks the killer wrongfully gained through murder.  These events combine to make up the Egyptian equivalent of the Iliad, and the battles that result are of epic importance.

Interestingly enough, this myth has survived in two versions with entirely different tones.  Many Egyptian myths have been told in different places and with different details, but this particular story has been recorded in versions so divergent as to lead to exactly opposite attitudes toward the central characters and events.  One version is entirely serious, even though it describes events that are fantastic.  Since this version is similar to the epics of the Western world (great battles, heroes fighting villains with gods taking an active role, supernatural events, and an oral tradition including repetition of key phrases), it is called here the epic version.

The other version presents a satiric view of the same characters.  In this "Parody" of the epic version (the reader should note that there is no proof which of the two versions was the first), the gods in the central roles are ridiculed and the battle is reduced to a petty squabble among deities who possess very human characteristics.

No evidence suggests that early Egyptians could not have held both the serious and humorous attitudes toward these events at the same time, since humor does not necessarily denote disrespect. The two accounts are separated here, however, in order to make the narratives and attitudes clearer.

## The Epic Version
## (briefly told)

The great battles between Horus and Seth began during the three hundred and sixty-third year of the reign of Ra-Herakhty on earth and ended decades later. Ra assembled a massive army in Nubia, in preparation for an attack on Seth who had rebelled against him. From a boat floating on the river he directed his troops of footmen, horsemen, and archers. Among them was Horus who had long sought to avenge his father's death but had been unable to trap Seth in battle; and so Horus, who loved an hour of fighting more than a day of feasting, looked forward to the battle with glee. Thoth gave the young god magic power to transform himself into a solar disk with large golden wings, the color of the sky at sunset; in this form Horus led Ra's troops into battle and prepared the tactics for the first encounter.

When Horus sighted the legions of Seth, he rose on his great wings above them and uttered a curse: "Your eyes shall be blinded and you shall not see; Your ears shall be deaf and you shall not hear." The enemy beneath him suddenly became confused: each warrior looked at the soldier next to him and, deceived by the power of the curse, saw a stranger where moments before an ally had stood. The speech around him sounded like a foreign language. The warriors cried out that their ranks had been infiltrated by the enemy, and they turned and fell upon each other. In a moment the army had defeated itself. Meanwhile Horus was hovering above, looking for Seth. His arch-enemy was not in this advance guard, but hiding in the marshes to the north. Horus continued to have trouble cornering Seth in battle, even though he was to chase Seth's troops through three more battles in the south and six in the north. Some took place in rivers, where the combatants changed themselves into crocodiles and

Plate 29.   The solar disk   *Horus*

Plate 30. Horus and Seth in battle

hippopotamuses, some took place on land where again the slaughter was terrible, and one was even fought on the high seas.

On one occasion when Horus thought he had captured his chief enemy during the heat of a battle, he cut off the soldier's head and severed the body into fourteen pieces as Seth had cut up Osiris. Once the dust from the battle settled, however, Horus finally saw his victim clearly and realized he had the wrong enemy: Seth had escaped him once again.

Later when Horus had matured, Seth challenged him to single combat. Isis decorated her son's boat with gold and prayed for his success (one is reminded of Achilles' mother's efforts in his behalf just before his great battle with Hector). Seth took the form of a red hippopotamus and prepared for battle at Elephantine Island in Aswan. With his great voice like thunder he used his power over storms as a terrible weapon. The waves and wind tossed Horus' boats about, but the young god stood fast at the prow and led his followers through the worst of the storm. At the point of blackest darkness the foam of the waters made the golden boat shine like the rays of the sun.

As the storms lessened, the two gods began their long-due battle which is said to have lasted three days. Somehow during the confusion Seth wrested Horus' left eye from his head, perhaps because he disguised himself as a black pig and tricked Horus into letting him get close. Horus redoubled his efforts and recaptured his eye, which later he was to feed to Osiris to ensure his eternal life. Horus revenged himself upon Seth for this injury by seizing the red god and pulling off his testicles.

At one point in the fighting Horus gained the upper hand and tied up his adversary. He asked Isis to guard Seth while he went in pursuit of the enemy army, but Seth tricked Isis with sweet words about her duty to her brother. Finally Isis felt so guilty she loosened Seth's ropes and allowed him to escape. When Horus discovered what had been done, he was so outraged that he cut his mother's head from her body with one blow of his knife. Fortunately Thoth was nearby and quickly replaced her missing head with the horns and solar disk of Hathor, which explains why in some depictions Isis wears Hathor's head and headdress.

With Seth at large again, Horus had to return to battle. A young god eight cubits tall (almost fourteen feet), he held a harpoon whose blade measured four cubits. He handled this mighty weapon as if it weighed no more than a reed. This time, when he sighted his long-time foe, he aimed with all his skill. The first cast caught the red hippopotamus full in the head and entered his brain. Finally, after years of battles, Horus had avenged the humiliation of his father, and Isis could rest.

## The Satiric Version

In the other version the action centers not on physical combat but on a court trial. Battles do occur, surely, but they are intertwined with some of mythology's more bizarre court scenes.

The gods assembled at Heliopolis as a court to hear the plea of young Horus against his uncle, Seth. Atum-Ra sat in the chair as chief judge, and Thoth was the main spokesman for the young god. The dilemma before the court was whether Horus should receive Osiris' position on earth because he was the blood heir, or whether Seth should receive it because he was stronger, older, and more fit to rule. Shu and others argued: "Justice should prevail over sheer strength. Deliver judgment saying 'Give the office to Horus.'"

But Atum-Ra was not happy. Fearing Seth's warlike character, and knowing that his retaliation if the case went against him would be more troublesome than anything Horus could attempt, he wanted to appease the red god and was angry with the court for giving in to Horus so easily. Seth then proposed that he and Horus resolve the issue through trial by combat, but Thoth asked the court if it would not be better to try to find out who was right and who was wrong rather than leaving the decision to a fight. The arguments before this court presented the classic case for civilization versus barbarism, a theme which runs throughout much of Egyptian mythology.

When Osiris asked if there were some approach other than combat, the gods decided that they were trying to settle the case with insufficient information, and that they would write to Neith, an ancient goddess renowned for her wisdom, to request her guidance. At once Thoth, as secretary of the gods, composed a letter which concluded: "What are we to do about these two fellows who have now been before the court for eighty years without our being able to decide between them? Please write and tell us what to do." Neith replied that the court should give Osiris' position to Horus, and mollify Seth by offering him a couple of minor goddesses to dally with. The court was pleased with this compromise and immediately decided Neith had great wisdom.

When Atum-Ra still refused to agree with the court, the other gods grew increasingly angry with him. Over the uproar, one god screamed at Atum-Ra: "Your shrine is empty!" Such an insult, of course, could not pass unnoticed; and Atum-Ra went sulking back to his house where he lay on his back without talking to anyone. Hathor, his daughter, saw that something had to be done for the old god and decided to tease him out of his ill humor. She danced in front of him, whipped up her gown, and suddenly bared her private parts before his startled eyes. Atum-Ra laughed out loud and returned to court in a better frame of mind.

He commanded the opponents to debate the matter in open court, where Seth and Horus repeated the old arguments. When the court agreed with Seth, Isis became angry and the court assured her that Horus would win the position. Seth, furious with his sister, told Atum-Ra that he would have nothing more to do with the court as long as Isis was around to influence it. Atum-Ra decided that a change in venue was in order and moved the court to an island. The ferryman, Anty, was ordered not to take Isis or anyone who looked like her across the water.

Isis, plotting to join the others on the island, disguised herself as an old woman with a bent back. Carrying a jar of barley and wearing a gold ring, she approached Anty and asked for a ride: "I have come for you to ferry me to Middle Island. I am taking a jar of barley to the little boy tending cattle there; he has been there five days and will be getting hungry." Anty protested that he was not supposed to ferry women, but she asked if his orders were not for Isis alone. Succumbing to temptation and believing it safe to help this old woman, he asked what she would give him if he consented. She offered some barley but he refused, declaring that he would not violate his orders just for some bread. She then offered the ring, and to no-one's surprise he took it.

Once on the island, she turned herself into a beautiful, seductive maiden. When Seth saw her, he left the court and called out from

Plate 31. Neith

behind a bush, "I would like to tarry here with you, fair child." Coyly she set her trap: "Ah, my great lord! I was married to a shepherd and bore him a son, but my husband died and the boy had to look after his father's animals. Then a stranger came and hid in the barn and told my son: 'I will beat you, take away your father's animals, and chase you away.' Now I want to persuade you to help my son." Seth, never known for his subtlety, and lusting after this fair creature, replied: "Indeed, should one give animals to a stranger while the man's son is at hand?" Isis immediately turned herself into a vulture and taunted her adversary from the branch of a tree: "Bewail yourself! Your own mouth has said it and your own judgment has judged you!" When Seth returned to court, even Atum-Ra had to agree that Seth had been tricked into foolishly judging himself. Anty nevertheless was sent for, and the court ordered that his lower legs be cut off as punishment; rumor tells that he "forswore the use of gold until the present day."

When the court appeared ready to award the position to Horus, Seth challenged his nephew to yet another contest. This time they were to change themselves into hippopotamuses and dive into the sea. Whoever held his breath under water for three months would be the winner. After the two gods had dived under, Isis, fearing that Horus would lose, decided to help him. Taking an ingot of bronze she forged it into the head of a harpoon to which she fitted a long shaft, making a fearful weapon. Then she took careful aim at Seth in the water and threw the harpoon with all her divine strength. The weapon went straight and pierced the sacred body of—Horus. With a cry of pain, he called his mother to remove the harpoon from his body. Regretting her mistake at once, she used her magic to free the harpoon and then cast once more at Seth and successfully held him fast. Seth in turn protested his treatment on the grounds that they too were flesh and blood. Moved by her brother's plea, Isis ordered the harpoon to release him. Horus was now angry again. He emerged from the water and cut off Isis' head with a knife that weighed sixteen bars. Their disagreement, however, did not last long, and soon she was back on his side.

Following this event there seems to have been a truce declared, and Horus and Seth went off to try to resolve the problem themselves. Actually this was another of Seth's tricks, for as soon as he was alone with the young god he raped him, in the hope that once the other gods

Plate 32. Seth in animal form

believed Horus was homosexual, they would repudiate him. Horus ran to his mother for help. She took some of his semen and dropped it on some lettuce (henceforth a symbol of sexual potency). When Seth unwittingly ate the seeds of Horus in a salad, he became pregnant by his nephew. Soon he went to the court with his charge of homosexuality, and the court at first laughed at Horus for his supposed weakness. He denied the charges and challenged the court to call up his seed. When summoned, the seed inside Seth grew into a large disk on his head; but before he could remove it, Thoth grasped it and placed it on his own head as a headpiece, which explains the origin of the disk on many later representations of Thoth. So the court sided with Horus.

As usual when he was about to lose the decision, Seth again challenged Horus to combat. This time he suggested a race in boats made of stone. Horus readily agreed; he made a boat of cedar covered with gypsum to give it the appearance of stone, and set it floating on the water. Seth saw that his nephew had successfully launched what appeared to be a stone boat and hurried about doing the same. He cut the peak off a mountain and used the stone to build a large boat. He launched it and watched as it promptly and surely sank to the bottom.

When the court intervened again and was about to award the position to Seth, Osiris finally made a plea on his son's behalf. This brought him into argument with Atum-Ra, but despite the chief god's words, and threats from Seth, the court changed its mind and decided in favor of Horus. Again Seth challenged Horus to combat, but by now even the court had had enough. Isis brought Seth into court bound in chains like a criminal. Atum-Ra asked him why he was not willing to allow the court to settle the case after eighty years. Much to everyone's surprise Seth agreed to end the fighting and permitted Horus to accept the position of Osiris awarded by the court. Brought before the court and placed on the throne of his father with Osiris' own crown, Horus was told that he was the master of every land for all eternity. (Part of the irony here lay in the fact that the "master of every land" had to be told he was master and given a crown; he was comically dependent on those he was supposed to rule.)

Ptah realized that justice was being done, but he also saw that Seth was being deprived of power that some believed he deserved. "What shall be done with Seth?" he asked. Atum-Ra quickly realized that he could make use of Seth's war-like nature and ordered Seth to stay beside him like a son: "He shall raise his voice in the sky and men shall be afraid of him." Thus Seth was given a permanent place, apparently in the solar boat, as the god of storms. There he intimidated men and protected Atum-Ra from his enemies.

# 7

# Hathor

The archetype of the Earth Mother is common to many mythologies; and at different times Isis, Sekhmet, and Nut—among others—have had this role in Egyptian mythology. Hathor, however, appears to have been the oldest example in Egypt and the prototype on which later ones were based. While substantial evidence of Hathor in this role exists from the earliest periods, R.T. Rundle Clark believes that during the Old Kingdom it was supressed or ignored, only to re-surface at the time of the Coffin Texts. By this time Isis and Nut had become important in their own right, and the texts contained an interesting version of creation in which all three goddesses in turn played the role of the Great Mother. The story contained a graphically gory account of the birth of Ihy, who was first called the son of Hathor, then of Isis; but Hathor dominated the myth.

Hathor's origin adds to the mystery about her roles. In the Coffin Texts she was called "the Primeval, the Lady of All, who lives on Truth," and claimed to have been created before the sky and earth. This myth told of her coming into existence at the time Ra rose as the sun god, when she took her place beside him in the solar boat. A variation, however, told that she was actually the daughter of Ra and Nut (we have seen that in some accounts they were lovers). When Hathor was born, she was said to have been either black-skinned or reddish-black. As a result of these birth myths (and of her association

110

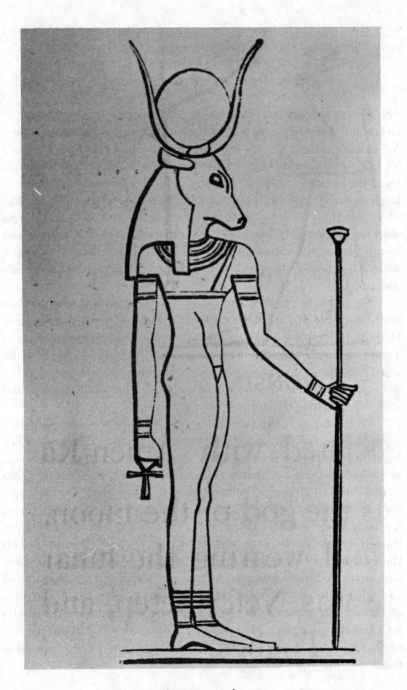

Plate 33.  Hathor

with Horus as the sun god) she was considered a sky goddess, and
wore the solar disk in her headdress.

## The Destruction of Mankind

The fullest account of the relationship between Ra and Hathor as
father and daughter came in another story from Ra's declining years.
As we have seen, in his old age Ra was grieved by a decline of respect
for him in the world he had created, and especially among the human
race, the product of his own tears. His human creations began to
laugh derisively at him: "Look at Ra! He is old and his bones are like
silver, his flesh is like gold, and his hair is like true lapis lazuli." Ra
objected to being called old; even the comparisons with precious
metals and stones called attention to the fact that his flesh was not
what it had been in his youth. He was angered by mankind's ridicule
and sought to teach them a lesson.

He called out to those followers who were close at hand and had
them assemble his nearest relatives: "Summon here my daughter
Hathor, the apple of my eye, and summon also the gods Shu and
Tefnut, Geb and Nut, and the great god Nun, whose dwelling is in the
waters of the sky." The messengers were instructed to summon the
gods quietly so that mankind would not guess what was happening and
seek refuge from the revenge being plotted.

At the mansion of Ra in the Hidden Place the gods and goddesses
assembled to find out what their father demanded of them. They
bowed down before him, touching the ground with their foreheads,
and asked their leader what he wanted them to do. Ra addressed Nun
as the eldest of all gods: "Behold the men whom I have created, how
they speak against me. Tell me what you think I should do to them,
for truly I will not slay them until I have heard your words." Even
though the last sentence suggests that the supreme god had decided on
the punishment before hearing the other gods' advice, Ra nevertheless
consulted his lesser colleagues. Nun, not surprisingly, told the chief
god what he wanted to hear. He suggested that Ra's eye in the form
of Hathor (the apple of her father's eye) be sent out to kill those who
attacked the great god. He reminded Ra that he was still the greatest
of the gods and his throne was secure: men should, therefore, have
much to fear from his anger.

The other gods quickly agreed to this simple strategy and Hathor was sent out in the form of Sekhmet, a fierce lioness, to seek revenge. She rushed to attack her prey and found that, like the lion, she took delight in slaughter. She discovered pleasure in shedding blood throughout the land and quickly taught Ra's tormentors that they should not laugh at the chief god. As she hastened to and fro, killing everyone she met, her father observed her work and at first was pleased. Soon he sensed that his vengeance was complete and called to her to stop before she eliminated the entire human race: "Come in peace, Hathor. Have you not done that which I gave you to do?" But there was no stopping her once she had tasted blood. She cried out, "By your life, O Ra, I work my will upon men and my heart rejoices."

For many nights the waters of the Nile ran red with the blood of mortals, and Hathor waded through blood until her feet became crimson. Ra took pity on mankind in spite of his former resentment, but no god or man could stop the ruthless carnage of the goddess who clearly enjoyed her role as lioness. Because of her divine power, no-one could force her to cease her killing, not even Ra himself; she had to be stopped by persuasion or trickery.

Unknown to Hathor, then, Ra asked for his swiftest messengers and sent them to Elephantine Island at Aswan with instructions to bring him a large quantity of the fruit of the mandrake, a plant that caused great sleepiness. Its fruit is crimson and scarlet and its juice is blood-red. After the messengers brought it to Ra in Annu with the swiftness of wind, the women there crushed barley and made beer mixed with the mandrake coloring to give it the appearance of blood. Working all night while Hathor rested, they made seven thousand measures of red beer and finished their task just as dawn broke. Ra and the other gods surveyed the night's work and felt pleased with themselves; Ra told the rest that he would use the brew to save mankind from total destruction, and sent his messengers out with orders to spread it over the earth.

Shortly Hathor arose and set out to continue her enjoyable task. She passed through the land looking for more prey to satisfy her thirst for blood, but saw none. Instead she saw that the earth was already deep in what appeared to be blood and rejoiced in the thought that she had spilled so much of the liquid of life. She stooped to drink of it, and found that the more she drank, the more she wanted. Finally the combination of the beer and the mandrake caused her to sink into a peaceful slumber. Her brain no longer urged her to kill, and her father quietly called to her: "Come, come in peace, O fair and gracious goddess." So ended her slaughter.

Ra went on to command that in future there would be celebrations of this event in the city of Amen, the place where the goddess was worshipped. Ra assured her and her followers that there would be three vases of beer for each of his handmaidens who participated in the festival of the New Year, and for generations the followers of Hathor were rewarded with an annual beer party. (One amusing scholarly explanation of this story is that it was devised to justify the excessive drinking that accompanied the yearly feast of Hathor.)

Ra, however, was not perfectly content with the outcome of events. He had found his revenge and had stopped it from being total so that mankind might survive, but he was still weary of man. He was also wary of the implications of what he had done, for he realized that for a time he, the greatest of the gods, had been unable to control his own daughter. He told Nun, "For the first time my limbs have lost their power, and I will never permit this thing to happen a second time."

*****

The oldest physical form given to Hathor was probably the cow. Sometimes she was depicted as the full animal; at other times as a woman with a cow's head. Sometimes she had a woman's body and face but was provided with a pair of horns encircling the solar disk. In the later form she can be confused with Isis who, as we have seen, was also given a cow's horns, or head, at times. At the temples of Dendera and Philae, her most important shrines, she was shown on the pillars as a woman with cow's ears. The face has an appealing smile and considerable beauty.

Her titles were many, but most of them reflected her connection with happiness and joy. In the broadest sense she represented what was good and true, and these traits were found in her characterization as a woman. She was the epitome of a wife, a daughter, a woman. She was the goddess of beauty, and in the Coffin Texts she said, "Come

114

Plate 34. Hathor as a cow in the mountains

with my horns and display my beauty; come with my face and I will cause you to be exalted." She was the goddess of love, music, dance, and singing. Artists revered her, as did drinkers of beer and wine.

In the Book of the Dead Hathor was also assigned a role in the underworld. At first, it seems, the role was not a prominent one: she was just one of the company of gods overseeing the soul's trial to attest to its fairness. Then she was thought of as provider of food and drink to souls making their way through the underworld. She was depicted as sitting within her sacred sycamore tree dispensing nourishment to the dead, who then sat and ate in its shade. By the twenty-first dynasty, however, her duties to the dead had been greatly expanded. In papyri from this period she is shown as the cow who greets the dead at the entrance to the Western Mountains, the location of the underworld. She is placed on the slope of the mountain with her pleasant head and horns protruding from the sand. In some of these papyri there is an interesting combination of myths: the cow as greeter of the dead was identified with the rising and setting sun. The ancient idea that Hathor represented the sky and was associated with the sun was here connected with her newer role in behalf of the dead at the entrance of the underworld. Her titles here were now "Lady of the West" and "Lady of the Holy Country." She was shown wearing a menat necklace: a beaded necklace that hung from the rear of the collar and was intended to symbolize regeneration and rebirth.

As one might expect, the goddess associated with love, beauty, and music and renowned as the Great Mother was celebrated widely in some of the most vivid rites recorded in ancient Egypt. Fairly early the murals showed her holding a sistrum, a musical rattle of metal and wood. It depicted a flattened face of Hathor with cow's ears and was used both for festive occasions and to frighten demons. Later she was celebrated in the Sacred Marriage.

## The Festival of the Sacred Marriage

The name of the cow goddess meant "the house of Horus," but the relationship between Hathor and Horus remains confused, in part because she was an Earth Mother and therefore associated with numerous other goddesses. In one important story Horus is Hathor's son. According to this myth Hathor was the cow whose legs held up the sky. Horus, as the sun god in the shape of a hawk, flew into her mouth every night and then was born again each morning.

There is, however, a surviving Ptolemaic ritual which was based on a different myth in which Hathor and Horus were husband and wife. The Sacred Marriage, one of the more elaborate Egyptian religious rituals, began on the eighteenth day of the tenth month when the image of Hathor was taken from her sanctuary at Dendera to sail up-river toward Horus' temple at Edfu. The goddess and her followers made numerous stops on the way, and reached Edfu on the day of the new moon toward the end of summer. There, on the eve of the anniversary of his victory over Seth, Horus left his temple and greeted his consort on the waters. The divine pair traveled by canal up to the temple amid numerous festivities, including the Opening of the Mouth and the offering of the First Fruits. This interesting combination of funerary and harvest rituals is probably the result of Horus' identification with Osiris, the god of both funerals and vegetation. That night the couple spent their time in the Birth Temple.

On the next day the celebration continued but with a different emphasis. This part was called the Festival of Behdet and consisted of rituals performed to assure the people of Horus' presence on the throne and his full authority. The activities included visits to the necropolis and ceremonies performed in behalf of the departed. A red ox and a red goat were sacrificed, and four geese were released to fly to the four corners of the earth announcing that Horus the Behdetite had again taken the crowns of Upper and Lower Egypt. Four arrows were shot to the four points of the compass to kill his enemies, and words of praise were said in his honor as the sun god: "Praise to you, Ra; praise to you, Khepri, in all these your beautiful names. You came here strong and mighty, have ascended beautiful, and have slain the dragon." His enemies were symbolically ravaged; fish, and models of a hippopotamus and a crocodile were trampled on while the names of his other enemies were inscribed on papyrus for all to know. Following the destruction of the enemies, the celebrants gave themselves up to a night of joy. At some point during the festival Horus and Hathor were intended to celebrate their marriage with a "beauteous embrace," and it can be assumed that this part of the ritual was a signal to the priests, priestesses, king, queen, and most of the commoners to do the same. Myth tells us that the mortals observed the festival by "drinking before the god" and "spending the night gaily," which was probably one of the chief reasons for the festival in the first place. After a fortnight of merriment Hathor was returned to her home at Dendera.

\*\*\*\*\*

Today in Upper Egypt the visitor will find numerous representations of Hathor in various historic sites. In the Temple of Seti I at Abydos she can be found greeting the king, and in the adjacent Temple of Ramesses II she was depicted suckling the young king. Just to the south Hathor had her chief cult center at Dendera. She was worshipped there long before the Ptolemaic temple was built at the site, but this temple, whose columns are embellished with her face, is the building most frequently associated with her. The inner walls show scenes of her worship. The sites at Luxor which depict Hathor are too numerous to describe here, but several important ones must be mentioned briefly. Hatshepsut's temple at Deir el Bahari from the eighteenth century contains a chapel dedicated to Hathor with numerous wall representations of the queen, her decendants, and Hathor. Actually the best of these representations has been moved to the Egyptian Museum in Cairo, where there is a sandstone chapel and a large and striking statue of Hathor as the cow, which shows her nursing the boy Amenophis II. Near Luxor at Deir el Medineh there is another chapel which commemorated Hathor's role in the birth of the royal children. At the museum in Luxor, among several representations of Hathor, is a beautiful wooden head of the cow, one of the most important artistic pieces found in the tomb of King Tutankhamun. Its horns are copper, its eyes—in the shape of the Eye of Horus—are lapis lazuli. The head and part of the neck are gilded, and the base of the neck is painted black to suggest the underworld in which she resided.

At Aswan Hathor had a temple at Philae, near another temple dedicated to Horus. This entire island complex, which was of course designed to honor Isis, demonstrated the association of these two important Earth Mothers. Finally, at Abu Simbel Ramesses II dedicated to Hathor the second of the two great temples built for his favorite wife, Nefertari, and images of the goddess are to be found inside.

# 8

# The Triad of Memphis

Today the ruins of Memphis lie a little over twenty kilometers to the southwest of modern Cairo. Not much is left of the old city, but at one time it was the capital of all Egypt and one of the most powerful cities in the world. Here, somewhere around the year 3000 B.C., the kings of the first dynasty forged a merger between the peoples of Upper and Lower Egypt and began to build a city worthy of their political achievements. It was a city for the living—full of houses, markets, government offices, and temples for worship of their gods—very little of which has survived. Its Egyptian name was Hikaptah, which meant "House of the Spirit of Ptah," and clearly indicated the town's dependence on its chief god.

Ancient Memphis was laid out around the Temple of Ptah. The temple, measuring about one-third by one-quarter of a mile, was the focal point of the town. The royal palace, called "The White Walls," was to the north, near the sacred lake and the royal gardens. To the south of the temple was the shrine of the Apis bull and stalls for the bull and his mother. A canal brought boats from the Nile to the town, which was bounded on both east and west by canals. The town probably covered an area about one and three-quarter miles long and three-quarters of a mile wide. In the nearby desert at Sakkara, the people built a city for their dead, which was ultimately to include the first pyramids and several important tombs.

Plate 35.  Apis bull

Of ancient Memphis little remains now, but scattered here and there are a few statues, including an interesting alabaster sphinx from the eighteenth dynasty. The most important piece is a limestone statue of Ramesses II which must have stood about thirteen meters high at one time. Now the legs and part of the crown are missing, and it lies on its back in a small museum where it can be examined, studied, photographed, and even touched. Nearby are the ruins of a temple and alabaster beds used to mummify the Apis bulls that were later buried in gigantic sarcophagi in Sakkara. These later items provide clues to the religious life of ancient Memphis.

## The Memphite Theology

The religious beliefs of Memphis are quite ancient, but according to Siegfried Morenz the gods of the area remained local until somewhere about the fifth and sixth dynasties. At this time the theological system of Heliopolis seems to have lost some influence, and the priests from Memphis took advantage of this to advance the power of their triad and insinuate them into the cosmology from Heliopolis. Jaroslav Cerny maintains that the theology of Memphis conflated the gods of Heliopolis into a system headed by its own god, Ptah, as first principle and creator. Rudolf Anthes has written: "The 'Memphite Theology' should be understood as the theological explanation and justification of the undisputed fact that Memphis was the residence of the kings. It was adapted to the concept current in Heliopolis, and was not designed for competition."

The politics of religion were potent. One text described the extent of Ptah's international political power as a result of his part in the creation:

> It was not the army that caused every nation to bring tribute...; it was the gods of the land of Egypt, the gods of every country, that caused the great princes of every country to bring tribute themselves to the King Ramessu... to convey their gold, their silver, their vases of malachite..., to bring their herds of horses, of oxen, of goats, of sheep.... It was not a prince that went to fetch them, it was not an army of

122

infantry that went to fetch them, it was not horsemen that went to fetch them. It was Ptah, father of the gods....

Through the centuries many gods were worshipped in Memphis, but Ptah emerged as their chief and the head of a triad that included his consort Sekhmet and their son Nefertem. The precise origin of Ptah remains unknown. Some scholars have evidence that he was originally a variation of the sun god, but other evidence suggests that he may equally have been connected with the moon; one prayer to him reads: "It is your two eyes that give light... your two eyes that circle day and night; your right eye is the disk of the sun, your left eye the moon. Your images are the indefatigable ones." Sir Flinders Petrie believed that Ptah was thought to be the incarnation of the Apis bulls which had long been worshipped at this site.

The theological beliefs from Memphis were recorded on a granite slab in the twenty-fifth dynasty (c. 710 B.C.), but the lost documents on which it was based were of the Old Kingdom, probably dating from about the same time as the Pyramid Texts. The inscription begins by identifying Ptah with Ta-Tenen, an ancient earth-god from Memphis, and with the king. Ptah is described as self-begotten and creator of the Nine Gods.

Next, the stone recalls the judgment of the Ennead which ended the war between Seth and Horus. At first the peace agreement gave Seth Upper Egypt and Horus the land of his father to the north, but eventually the two were pacified and united in the House of Ptah. Horus came to be lord of both Upper and Lower Egypt, which made Ptah supreme god since Horus was an ingredient of Ptah, a point of doctrine which is confusing theologically but politically serviceable.

In the following section, the stone acclaims Ptah as supreme god and creator of all: "For the very great one is Ptah, who gave life to all the gods and their *kas* through his heart and through his tongue...." The text recalls the widely recognized version of creation from Heliopolis that claimed Atum created the Ennead through masturbation, but it makes the higher claim that Ptah spoke the words that inspired Atum's action. Ptah's heart was the seat of intelligence and his tongue the agent of the heart: "For every work of the god came about through what the heart devised and the tongue commended." In addition to creating the gods, Ptah was the originator of food, provisions, divine offerings, justice, labor, movement of the body—"all good things," as the text said. Ptah was acknowledged as the mightiest of the gods, and it was said of him that he "was satisfied after he had made all things and all divine words."

The text then concludes by asserting Memphis' claim to be the royal city because it was located at the spot where Isis and Nephthys brought Osiris to land after his drowning by Seth.

## PTAH

In his usual depiction, Ptah was one of the most distinctive of all the gods. He was shown as a bald-headed man, wearing a beard and a tight-fitting garment reminiscent of a mummy's wrappings; from the back of the neck hung a flower-shaped menat, symbol of happiness. His hands protruded from the front of the garment and held a scepter made up of three symbols: the long pole scepter (strength), the ankh (life), and the djed pillar (stability). In many of his depictions he was standing on the platform associated with Maat who represented truth and justice. He was called "Lord of Maat, king of the two lands, the god of the Beautiful Face in Thebes, who created his own image, who fashioned his own body, who has established Maat throughout the two lands."

As seen in the theology described above, one of Ptah's dominant roles was that of creator. He was described as the god "who has made all gods, men, and animals; he who has created all lands and shores and the ocean in his name 'fashioner of the earth.' " As heart and tongue of the Ennead, he was both the origin of intelligence and the means of communicating it. He was both the spokesman who issued the words and the artisan who forged part of the creation. As a result, Ptah was the Patron of all those who create handicrafts and work with metal or stone. He was the great artificer of Egyptian mythology.

Ptah was later to be associated with numerous other gods, especially Sokaris and Osiris, both of whom were connected with death. His mummy-like dress further emphasized his role in behalf of souls in the underworld. Ptah was considered "Lord of the Years"—measurer of time, but timeless himself: "I am yesterday, today, and tomorrow for I am born again and again. I am the Lord of

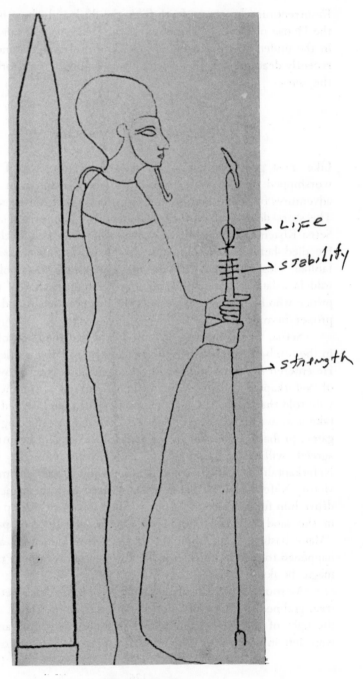

Life

stability

strength

Plate 36.　Ptah

Resurrection who comes forth from the dusk and whose birth is from the House of Death." The Book of the Dead makes Ptah responsible in the underworld for using an iron knife to open the mouth of the recently dead person, an act which was supposed to restore the use of the senses.

### Ptah as Royal Protector

Like most gods, Ptah was also viewed as protector of those who worshipped him. A tale from a Ptolemaic manuscript relates the adventures of Setna, Ptah's chief priest during the nineteenth dynasty. The story deals with historical characters—Ramesses II and his son Setna Khaemuast, who was a worthy soldier as well as chief priest. He died before his father and was buried at Sakkara. This moral fabliau, closely linked with the one concerning the Book of Thoth told in a later chapter, presents a rather human view of the famous prince who had to learn to respect the power of magic and to practice proper humility.

Setna, the high priest of Ptah, heard that the Book of Thoth lay in the tomb of Neferkaptah, the prince who had died while stealing it. He entered the tomb and found the magic book lying between the *kas* of Neferkaptah and his wife. When Setna asked for the book, the wife told the tragic tale of their sacrifice for it and begged him not to take it away. When Setna persisted, Neferkaptah challenged him to a game, probably senet, the board-game of the ancient Egyptians. Setna agreed willingly, thinking he could easily win the book; but Neferkaptah put a spell on him and beat him time after time. At each victory Neferkaptah hit Setna over the head with the game-board and drove him further into the ground. Soon the priest was up to his neck in the sand and called to his brother who had accompanied him, "Make haste and go upon the earth, and tell the king all that has happened to me, and bring me the talisman of my father Ptah, and my magic books."

As soon as the talisman was placed on his head, Setna jumped free, grabbed the Book of Thoth, and ran from the tomb. As he did, the light of the tomb went with him and Neferkaptah and his wife were left in darkness. When Setna displayed the book to Ramesses, the king warned him of its dangers; but the high priest unrolled the book and read it to all who would listen.

Later, while walking through the Temple of Ptah at Memphis, Setna spied a beautiful woman. He sent a servant to inquire about her and soon discovered she was Tabubu, daughter of a priest of Bast, and had come to worship Ptah. Boldly Setna sent the servant back with an offer of ten pieces of gold if she would sleep with him. The woman replied that she was a lady of rank but that if Setna came to her home at Bubastis there would be no risk of discovery.

By boat Setna hastened to his rendezvous. Once he found her house, he was conducted upstairs to a richly decorated room with both dining tables and couches. He and Tabubu spent the day in agreeable discourse and feasting, but the more Setna observed her beauty, the more he hungered not for her food but her personal delights. When he begged her to yield to his desire, she reminded him that she was a lady of rank, and said she would consent to his wishes only if he would sign a letter promising to maintain her and to make over all his property to her. Without hesitation he called for a scribe and signed away his worldly wealth.

Tabubu put on a diaphanous robe that clearly revealed her promised charms. Setna's desire grew more impatient, and shrewdly Tabubu used her advantage. She ordered his children be summoned, in order that they might sign the letter too. Without hesitation Setna made his own children add their names to the document giving up their birth-right.

Inflamed with passion, he then turned to Tabubu for relief, but once again she held him back. "Now kill your children," she ordered, "so that they cannot fight with my own children over your property." Too far gone to stop now, he had his own sons and daughters slain and their bodies thrown out of the window. As the dogs in the street tore at their tender flesh, their father sought his satisfaction. Tabubu led him to a bed of ivory and ebony. He undressed, exposing his physical excitement. As last he was about to claim the promised joys for which he had paid so dearly. He reached out to take her in his arms and suddenly she let out a scream. In an instant he found himself alone, naked, and aroused. It was as though he had awakened from a dream.

127

At that moment Ramesses happened to ride by and Setna knew he ought to stand up out of respect, but his physical condition made him embarrassed to do so. The king nevertheless saw his son and chided him: "Why are you in this shameful state?" Setna finally understood that Neferkaptah had enchanted him, and told his father the story. Ramesses advised him to return to Memphis where he would find his children unharmed. He also suggested that his men clothe the self-conscious prince.

After Setna was reunited with his children, Ramesses reminded him he had been warned not to take the Book of Thoth. The only salvation was to return it and do penance.

When Ptah's chief priest re-entered the tomb, bearing the book, Neferkaptah's wife was overjoyed to see him although the two *kas* had obviously relished his discomfiture. She told the high priest, "It is Ptah, the great god, who has brought you back safe." Her husband was less kind, remarking: "It is your own fault; this is what I warned you about before." As a penance Neferkaptah sent Setna to find the bodies of his wife and son and bring them to join their spirits in his tomb. Once he had accomplished this task and placed the book between husband and wife, the tomb was again filled with light.

## SEKHMET

Ptah's consort, Sekhmet, was called the "Great Lady, beloved of Ptah, holy one, powerful one." She was both wife and sister to Ptah, a common situation in Egyptian mythology. Usually she was depicted with the body of a woman and the head of a lioness. Her headpiece consisted of a solar disk, which associated her with the sun god, and a uraeus (or cobra); and she was often dressed in red. Her physical description and her name, which meant "to be strong, mighty, violent," reflected her character: she was renowned for her violence and power. The Book of the Dead attributed her power to her use of the destructive forces of the sun's heat and also associated her with the hot winds of heaven. Other sources associated the hot winds of the desert with her breath. She was a goddess of war and accompanied the king into battle—her weapons were arrows, swift darts, and the fiery heat of her own body which supposedly derived

Plate 37.  Sekhmet

from the heat of the sun. She said of herself: "I am the fierce heat of the fire for a distance of millions of cubits between Osiris and his enemy, and I keep away from him the evil ones and remove his foes from his habitation." Apparently her power was great enough not only to assist Osiris but at times to dominate even him; according to the Book of the Dead, at the times of storms and great floods she had power even over the great god of the underworld.

Sekhmet's father was said to have been Ra himself, and many of her attributes connected her with the sun god. In the early Egyptian writings she was often called the Eye of Ra, which was supposed to have represented the god when he was forced to take action against his enemies and was vindictive and fierce — the traditional evil eye. Judging from the hieroglyph for this eye, we can assume that its power was derived from the combativeness of the uraeus and the heat of the sun. As we saw in Chapter Seven, when Ra sent Hathor out to avenge his mistreatment by men, he sent her in the form of Sekhmet, the lioness. This merging of the two goddesses accentuates the fact that in later years Sekhmet was connected with the character of numerous other goddesses, including Hathor, Nut, and Baset (who as a domestic cat was sometimes said to represent the gentler aspect of Sekhmet). Amenhetep III placed several hundred statues of her in his temple dedicated to Mut at Karnak.

There were two minor characteristics of this goddess that seem at odds with her predominantly violent nature. First, she was often depicted holding or carrying the ankh, the sign of life; and second, she was renowned for her role as a healer because of her knowledge of magic and sorcery. These indications of care and concern for others are not easily reconciled with what else is known about her activities.

## NEFERTEM

The last of the triad of Memphis—as it was constituted in Pharaonic times—Nefertem was an unlikely son of Ptah and Sekhmet, for his demeanor was quite the opposite of his mother's. The texts found in the pyramid of Unas at Sakkara associated him with the lotus flower: "Unas has risen like Nefertem from the lotus to the nostrils of Ra, and he goes forth from the horizon on each day, and the gods are

Plate 38.  Nefertem

sanctified by the sight of him." Later the Book of the Dead was to confirm this picture of Nefertem. He seems to have been the god of fragrance or perfume, charged with preventing offensive odors from reaching the solar god during his passage each day through the sky. His mild manner was mirrored in the prayers spoken to him by the dead. As part of the ritual of purification before entering eternal life, the souls addressed the gods singly, pleading their innocence of some forty-two grievous sins. The prayer to Nefertem demonstrates respect for his lack of guile: "Hail, Nefertem, who comes forth from [Memphis]; I have not acted with deceit, and I have not worked wickedness."

Aside from these few references, not much is known about the child of the chief parents of Memphis. The usual representation of him was that of a man holding an ankh and wearing lotus blossoms on his head. Sometimes he was depicted standing on a recumbent lion or with a lion's head; the lotus head-dress was invariable. The treasures of King Tutankamun include a wooden statue of the boy king emerging as the god Nefertem from a lotus flower.


## IMHOTEP

During later dynasties Ptah and Sekhmet were credited with parenthood of a historical figure, Imhotep (variant spellings: Imhetep and Iemhetep). There is continuing debate over whether or not Imhotep supplanted Nefertem in the Memphis triad; it seems that the triad consisted of the gods already described here until the Graeco-Roman period, when Imhotep replaced Nefertem.

It was an established belief that when any king died he became a god, but Imhotep is a striking example of the deification of a man of lower rank. He was the chief advisor to King Zoser early in the third dynasty (c. 2686 B.C.). He designed and built the funerary complex at Sakkara; specifically he is credited with being the architect for the Step Pyramid, built for Zoser. One story of his advice survives. In a famous myth associated with the god Khnum (to be told in detail in Chapter Ten), a king, who may well have been Zoser, went to Aswan to consult the god about a continuing famine that racked the country. It was said that his journey was made on the advice of Imhotep.

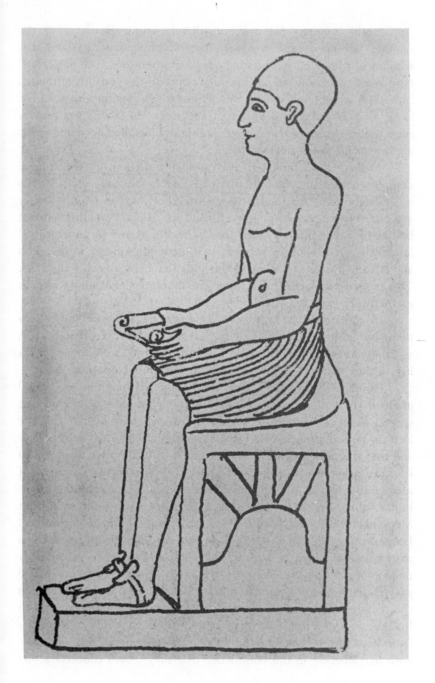

Plate 39.   Imhotep

Apparently Imhotep did not immediately know the cause of the famine, but he consulted his books and came to understand that Khnum was angered by the king's lack of attention. The prescribed cure was for the king to pay his due tribute to the god. Even though Imhotep was remembered for this service to his king, he also achieved fame as a magician and healer of the sick. In later years he was renowned for his work as a physician though detailed accounts of his medical work have not survived.

At his death Imhotep was probably buried in the funeral complex at Sakkara, but his tomb has yet to be discovered. It has been established that the ibis sacred to Thoth was in later dynasties associated with Imhotep as well, and at Sakkara the mummified bodies of half a million ibises have been discovered in underground labyrinths. It is thought that the sick made pilgrimages to his tomb and left the ibises as offerings in the hope that he would cure their ills. The birds were wrapped in beautiful mummy linens and sealed in earthenware pots.

In the centuries following his death he achieved status as a demigod with special medical powers. It is possible that he was worshipped as early as the fourth dynasty, and in the following years his shrines were visited by people seeking miraculous cures.

About two thousand years after his death Imhotep was raised gradually to the full status of a god, although there is no record of a special ritual or moment of deification. It may have been during the Persian period after 525 B.C. that Imhotep was granted full divinity and that after this time he was worshipped with complete honors until four centuries after the birth of Christ. He was recognized as a god of medicine, and a school of medicine and magic was established in his honor at a hospital at Memphis. Temples were built to him at Memphis, Philae, and Thebes where sick people came to be cured. A late story provides an example of his curative powers. There lived a man who had no male heirs by his wife, and the two were deeply unhappy as a result. The wife went to a temple of Imhotep and prayed that he work a miracle in their behalf. That night she slept in the temple and dreamed of a message from the god. She was told to find the root of a particular plant, the colocasia, and make a medicine from it to give to her husband. Once that was done, she should lie with her husband in full confidence that they would conceive a boy child that night. She did as the dream instructed, and the resulting heir became a remarkable man long remembered for his wonderful powers.

Imhotep's name meant "he who comes in peace," appropriate for a god who brought so much wisdom and healing to mankind. Since he was remembered for both wisdom and healing, he was often associated with Thoth, the god of wisdom who was also connected with medicine during the earlier dynasties. Imhotep was supposed to be the god who sent sleep to those in great pain and suffering. He was believed to treat men's illnesses while they were alive, and help prepare their bodies for eternal life after their death.

At Philae there survives a small temple in his honor, and a Greek inscription over the door from the reign of Ptolemy V shows the respect still shown to this former mortal quite late in the Graeco-Roman period: Imhotep was called the "great one, son of Ptah, the creative god, made by Thenen, begotten by him and beloved by him, the god of divine forms in the temples, who gives life to all men, the mighty one of wonders, the maker of times, who comes unto him that calls upon him wheresoever he may be, who gives sons to the childless, the wisest and most learned one, the image and likeness of Thoth the wise."

Surviving statues of Imhotep also come from the late period. He was depicted like Ptah, with a bald head, and he was usually shown in a seated position with an open roll of papyrus on his knees, the traditional position for scribes in ancient Egypt.

*****

Worship of the triad obviously began at Memphis, where the temple to Ptah was probably the most celebrated building in the ancient city. Different kings contributed to its splendor up through the twenty-sixth dynasty. Ramesses II, as was his custom elsewhere, made sure that he was well represented there and added two statues of himself at the entrance to the temple; one is now lying partly broken at Memphis; the other stands in front of the railway station in central Cairo, where sadly the fumes from the cars, trucks and buses at this, one of the most congested areas in Cairo, are eating away at the stone. Not much remains now of the Temple of Ptah in Memphis, but a few of the ruins can be studied, showing some interesting wall carvings and the outlines of the temple itself. For a god as important as Ptah, however, worship would not have been restricted to a single temple, and there is evidence throughout Egypt of his veneration. To the south at Abydos the Temple of Seti I included a vaulted chamber dedicated to the worship of Ptah and adorned with murals describing the ceremonies which the king was obliged to perform in Ptah's honor. In Luxor King Thothmes III dedicated a temple within the Karnak complex and, as we have seen, the Temple of Mut there contained statues of Sekhmet. Local gossip tells that, in modern times, one of the statues killed and ate some of the village children, and rumor has it that the women of the city still admonish their children to be good or they will be eaten by the statue. There is another statue of Ptah in the far south of Egypt, in the Great Temple of Ramesses II at Abu Simbel, and it is evident that he was worshipped there alongside Amun-Ra. Of course the Egyptian Museum in Cairo contains statues and other representations of the triad and of Imhotep, especially in the Tutankhamun exhibit. The museum also contains statues of the Apis bulls who were associated with Ptah, and the one surviving mummy of the bulls lies in the Agricultural Museum in Cairo.

# 9

# The Triad of Thebes

Nearly seven hundred kilometers south of Memphis lay the tiny village which today has become the goal of visitors from all over the world because of the remarkable ruins. Called Luxor now it was known as Thebes during its period of dominance, and as Waset before that, when it was an almost unknown village along the banks of the Nile. Thebes was an important town of Upper Egypt during the early Pharaonic dynasties, but during the Middle Kingdom (c. 2133-1786 B.C.) it became the political and religious center of Egypt. Its later kings led invasions into Asia and Africa, and with their plunder built a city worthy of men who ruled the civilized world.

Each district in the area worshipped its own gods: Wast was the goddess of Waset, Montu was worshipped nearby, and Amun was the local deity of another village somewhat to the north. Amun was at first a variation of Min, the ithyphallic god worshipped in Koptos; but by the twelfth dynasty, followers of Amun gained political ascendancy and made their god the chief of all the area. He was to form the triad of Thebes, along with Mut, his consort, and Khons, their son; and he was said to head a college of thirteen gods. His influence spread, and by the eighteenth dynasty his characteristics had assumed those of Ra as the sun god, and a great single national god—Amun-Ra—was formed. He was an amalgamation of numerous sun gods, by whatever names the god was called; as a composite divinity he did not have a unique theology. Most of the myths associated with him were those that earlier had been identified with Ra: he was considered chief of the gods, uniter of the Two Lands of Upper and Lower Egypt, creator of all things including mankind and all other gods, captain of the solar boat, judge of the gods, defender of his eye, and victor over Apophis. Clearly these myths were old ones assumed by the priests of Amun-Ra at the time of his ascendancy. Amun did, however, have a distinct personality and visual depiction, which deserve treatment, and there are several myths reserved for this important god of all the nation.

## AMUN

Like Ra, his peer from the north, Amun was identified as the sun god who created the universe and was the source of all life. In his most elemental form he can be found in the creation myth of Hermopolis (see Chapter Ten), where he and his female partner, Amaunet, represented the air, as two of the group of gods who gave shape to the world. Eventually Nun, the primeval ocean, was absorbed into the concept of Amun, perhaps (in the view of Siegfried Morenz) because the people preferred a system of creation in which there was both a specific act of creation and a divine figure, such as Amun, responsible for it.

As a national god, Amun was believed to have important political duties as protector of the king and guarantee of success against enemies. A fragment from the period of the Ramesses kings tells of the attempts of the Hyksos king Apohis to disrupt the empire of the Theban ruler Seknenre (the entire mansucript was perhaps intended to advance Amun-Ra's prestige). Apohis, a follower of Seth, observed that Seknenre relied only on Amun-Ra, king of the Gods, and he designed a test of the god's power and willingness to protect his prince. Apohis sent a messenger to Seknenre complaining that the nightly noises of the hippopotamuses in a nearby canal kept him awake and he asked the king to see that he got some sleep. Unfortunately the king's solution to the problem was lost along with the rest of the manuscript, but Amun's responsibilities for his earthly kingdom are clear.

Further evidence of the belief in the bountiful grace of Amun toward the king is found in the story of "The Taking of Joppa," from

Plate 40.    Amun-Ra

the reign of Thutmose III. Earlier the king had defeated Joppa (modern Jaffa), but later the city rose up in rebellion. Thutmose sent his general Djehuty to retake the city, and the general arranged to parley with the rebel leader outside the city. Once alone with the rebel, Djehuty took his king's cane, which he had brought into battle, and smote the man on the forehead while testifying aloud that Thutmose's strength came from Amun. Once the leader had been captured, Djehuty set about taking the city. He deceivingly sent word to the city that Djehuty had fallen and was delivering tribute. Djehuty's soldiers then hid in two hundred baskets which were taken to the city as peace offerings. Once brought inside the city, the men escaped from the baskets and quickly subdued the rebels (the ruse of hiding soldiers inside a present is here about two centuries older than the story of the Trojan horse). Djehuty then sent a message to his king which gave Amun credit for the victory: "Be of good cheer! For Amun, your good father, has given to you the rebel of Joppa and all his people, likewise also his city. Send men to take them away as captives that you may fill the house of your father Amun-Ra, King of the Gods, with male and female slaves, who have fallen beneath your feet forever."

Amun was usually depicted as a ram with curved horns, a man with a ram's head, or a man with two upright plumes as a headpiece. Herodotus explained how this association with the ram came about in a myth that also explained the meaning of the name Amun—"The Hidden One." The Greek traveler claimed that the Egyptians had told him a story in which Khons wanted to see what his father looked like, but Amun was reluctant to grant this special favor even to his own son. Amun had heretofore hidden his appearance from everyone, but when Khons persisted with his request, Amun devised a trick to satisfy the son and still not reveal all his secrets. He skinned a ram and cut off its head. Just before showing himself to Khons, he covered himself with the skin and put the ram's head in front of his own face. All the young god saw was the likeness of a ram. According to Herodotus, this myth explained why Egyptians revered and refused to sacrifice the ram, except once a year when, in celebration of this story, they killed one ram and used the skin to clothe a statue of Amun just before it was revealed to a statue of Khons.

According to the famous Harris papyrus from the reign of Ramesses III, an inventory of Amun's great wealth listed "5,000 divine statues, more than 81,000 slaves, vassals, and servants, well over 421,000 head of cattle, 433 gardens and orchards, 691,334 acres of land, 83 ships, 46 building yards, and 65 cities and towns." Obviously this wealth could only have been accumulated by a god of wide influence. Possibly as a result of Amun's association with the air and wind, he came to be seen as the patron of mariners; he was the "pilot who knows the water." A hymn told of Amun's great power on the waters: even the crocodile feared the mention of his name. His aid to mariners extended to help for all in distress, and Amun gained wide respect as the god to whom anyone could turn for assistance. As a result he was worshipped by king and commoners alike; he was a national god and a personal god at the same time. Connected with this concept was the idea that he controlled the lifespan of individuals. He could lengthen or shorten a life, and was known to give additional years to those he loved.

## Amun-Ra as Divine Parent

Amun's involvement in human life is well illustrated by a myth taken from the walls of the Birth House at Deir-el-Bahri, the great temple of Hatshepsut. Kings were believed to assume their divine nature as a result of having been conceived by the chief god. For Hatshepsut this myth had additional value, for she was a woman king complete with false beard. Both ambition and ability took her beyond the limited roles normally assumed by women at the time, and through means both fair and foul she usurped the throne in the eighteenth dynasty. Justifying her action was, therefore, unusually important, and she took care that her temple fully recorded her divine paternity.

Amun-Ra met in council with the most powerful and important gods to seek their advice. They had to settle the succession to the crown, and Amun-Ra announced that he was to father the next heir to the throne, a child whose name was to be Hatshepsut. Plans were made for Amun-Ra to seduce the consort of the reigning king. Thoth identified the woman as Aahmes, renowned for her great beauty, wife of Thutmose I, king of Upper and Lower Egypt. Amun-Ra assumed

141

the shape of the husband so as to obtain his way without dispute or force, and Thoth led him to the mortal woman. Not suspecting that a god walked before them in disguise, the guards at the palace allowed what they thought to be the king to pass into the queen's rooms.

She lay asleep on her bed and her sensual form aroused him. Disturbed, she awoke to see the figure of her husband before her and she eagerly welcomed him to her bed. Amidst divine passion the future king of all Egypt was conceived.

Once satisfied, Amun-Ra rose to depart, but his ego, which was as large as the universe he ruled, would not let him maintain the deception. He had to tell the woman who he really was. Knowing then that she had been seduced by the King of the Gods and the Lord of the Thrones of the Two Lands, Aahmes proudly acquiesced and accepted his favors and power. She told him that she welcomed the union of her majesty and his glory. He replied, "I have made you pregnant and Hatshepsut will be the name of the daughter you will bear. She will be king of the Two Lords and will rule with my authority and protection."

Amun-Ra then left the queen and went to Khnum, the god known for creating humans of clay on his potter's wheel. Amun-Ra ordered Khnum to shape the future king out of the spirit of the chief god's own body and claimed to have already given the child health, strength, wealth, happiness, and eternal life. Khnum gladly responded, "I shall perform the deed and she will be more wonderful than the gods."

Khnum then sat in front of his potter's wheel and created two figures; one was Hatshepsut and the other her ka. Beside him was Heget, the frog-headed goddess, whose job it was to breathe life into the figures. Khnum talked to the girl he was creating: "I am forming you of the substance of Amun, god of Karnak. I give you the lands of Egypt and her people, and I will have you appear in glory as king in the role of Horus. You will be supreme among men, as has been commanded by your father, Amun-Ra."

Amun-Ra then sent Thoth, messenger of the gods, to Aahmes to tell her of the chief god's pleasure with her conception. As reward, Thoth presented special titles that made her stand out from other women.

Plate 41. Bes

As her time approached, Aahmes walked to the birth house escorted by Heget and Khnum who told the woman that her child would be greater than any king who had lived before her. Amun-Ra himself led the joyful group into the special rooms.

Once inside she was greeted by Meskhent, goddess of birth. Close by was Bes, divine protector of new mothers and newborn children, as well as god of music, dance, and jollity. Popular among kings and commoners alike, he was recognized as protector of domestic happiness, encourager of toilet training, and even at times the supervisor of the bed and its pleasures. He was a bow-legged dwarf with a roundish face and large, animal-like ears. His nose was wide and flat, his eyebrows prominent, and his face heavily bearded; but in place of hair on top of his head, he usually had feathers. His grotesque appearance was intended to frighten away snakes and other creatures who threatened Bes' human charges.

The birth was an easy one; the assistance of all these divinities had assured Aahmes that all would go well. Soon she was seated holding the infant who would seek so much of the known world. The goddesses present offered Hatshepsut the ankh, the sign of life, and Meskhent granted her the attributes that would make her happy as a woman.

Next Hathor presented the baby to her immortal father. As the cow goddess held out the child, Amun-Ra blessed his offspring, "You will be king of all Egypt and will sit on the throne of Horus. Welcome, child of my own body." Hatshepsut was suckled by a cow-headed goddess; Anubis rolled a disk to determine the length of her reign. Once weaned, she was served by Iat, goddess of milk, and guarded by other goddesses who took special interest in their important charge. The girl was finally taken back to Amun-Ra, who was accompanied by Thoth. Together they inspected the growing girl and approved her progress. As a final act of charity, Amun-Ra again granted her life, strength, health, wealth, and eternal life on the throne.

\*\*\*\*\*

A god of such power was honored widely and magnificently. Wall carvings at the Temple of Luxor describe in detail rituals

Plate 42. The rays of Aten descending toward Ikhnaton (Amenhotep IV) and his wife Nefertiti

performed in Amun's honor each year during the Festival of Opet. At the height of the flood Amun was taken from his residence at the Temple of Karnak to visit his female friends at the Temple of Luxor several hundred meters to the south. The festival opened with dancing girls who accompanied the priests of Amun as they carried the barge holding the statue of the god to the water's edge. Then men towed the barge up river to the other temple while the audience clapped, animals were sacrificed, and acrobats tumbled joyously. Finally at the second temple, offerings were made to the holy triad of Thebes.

The great seat of Amun's worship was, of course, the Temple of Karnak. The largest religious shrine in the world, it was begun during the twelfth dynasty and added to and modified by every ambitious king up to the Graeco-Roman period. One king would decorate a temple, another would build a courtyard, others added the wall, and Hatshepsut erected two obelisks. Here Amun-Ra was worshipped in a grandeur known to no god before him, and few since.

The worship of Amun was interrupted in one of the more curious theological events of ancient Egypt. Amenhetep IV, also known as Ikhnaton, gave Egypt a brief period of monotheism during which he made every effort to stop the worship of Amun. He moved his capital to Tel el Armarna, north of Luxor, and put his faith in the worship of Aten (variant spelling: Aton) who was envisioned as the sun. Ra and Amun were seen by their followers as personifications of the sun, but Amenhetep IV rejected the personalized god in favor of a less human deity. He discouraged the adoration of the god in human form and substituted the worship of the sun's rays. The worship of Aton was short-lived and within a few years Amun was reinstated under the guidance of the boy king, Tutankhamon, who set about restoring the monuments of Amun defaced during the period of "heresy." Some artifacts connected with the worship of Aten can be found in the Egyptian Museum, and the ruins of Tel el Armarna can be visited about sixty-seven kilometers south of Minia.

## MUT

Amun's consort at Thebes was Mut, whose name means "mother." She was considered a great world-mother who conceived all things

146

Plate 43.  Mut

and brought them into existence. She was usually drawn in the form of a woman, and she wore the double crown of Upper and Lower Egypt. In her hands she held a papyrus scepter and an ankh. She was associated with the vulture, which was supposed to indicate that she was a protective goddess; and the hieroglyphics for her name contained this bird. Often the vulture sits on her head under the double crown, but in the Book of the Dead there is a drawing that probably represents Mut, in which she stands with arms outstretched and covered with vulture's wings. Beside her head are the heads of two vultures. The same chapter of the Book of the Dead associated her with dwarfs, and it was said that she made souls and bodies strong and delivered them "from the abode of the fiends which is in the evil chamber." She was also identified with Maat, and in some representations she was shown standing beside Maat's plume.

The best-known seat of worship for Mut was her own temple at Karnak. Built about 1450 B.C. by Amenhetep III, this small temple is today in ruins, but at one time it was constructed around two inner courtyards, packed with over six hundred black granite statues of the goddess Sekhmet, and it was here that Ptah's consort from Memphis was associated with her Theban counterpart. There were other shrines to Mut from Upper Egypt to the Delta.


## KHONS

The son of Mut and Amun was Khons, whose name probably meant "to travel, to move about, to run." Amun had sometimes been refered to as The Traveler, but it was his son who was assigned duties as the messenger of the gods. He was associated with Thoth, who also served as a divine messenger at times; and because of this connection Khons was thought of as a god of the moon. In one of his forms he caused the crescent moon to shine upon the earth. In this capacity he helped women conceive children, cattle become fertile, and filled the nostrils and throats of living creatures with the air of life.

The typical representation of Khons showed him as a man with the head of a hawk, and often on his head he wore a lunar disk sitting in the crescent moon. One of the more interesting representations of him was as a man with double hawks' heads, one for the sun and the

Plate 44.  Khons

other for the moon. He had four vulture wings and stood on the heads of a pair of crocodiles.

The priests of ancient Egypt used numerous devices to encourage belief in the gods and maintain a steady flow of offerings. One such practice was the oracle, through which the god spoke words of wisdom to supplicating humans who came for advice. At Kom Ombo, for instance, one can see an underground tunnel used by the priests to transmit the voice of the "god" from the inner sanctuary, where no one went but the high priest, to the front where the suppliant awaited the god's message. Carvings on a stone stele tell of a similar device used to enhance the power of Khons. The form of Khons involved in this myth was known as Khons Neferhetep, who was supposed to have complete power over the evil spirits of the air who caused pain, sickness, and death. There was a distant country called Bekhten which lay so far from Egypt the journey there took seventeen months, but even so the prince of Bekhten married his eldest daughter to the king of Egypt, thereby creating special ties between the two countries. Some time later the prince himself paid a visit to the court in Thebes and told the king that his younger daughter, the sister of Egypt's queen, was seriously ill. None of the treatments prescribed in Bekhten had been effective and the prince asked that an Egyptian physician be sent to treat the girl. When the physician arrived, he discovered that his patient was under the influence of an evil spirit; and since his medicine had no effect on the spirit, he eventually admitted defeat. The prince then returned to Thebes to ask for new assistance.

When the king of Egypt heard the details of the problem, he went to the temple of Khons Neferhetep and prayed: "O my fair lord, I have come once again to pray to you on behalf of the daughter of the prince of Bekhten." The king begged the god Khons himself to go to the country to deal with this extraordinary illness: "Grant that your magical power may go with him and let me send his divine majesty into Bekhten to deliver the daughter of the prince of that land from the power of the demon." This prayer was made in front of a statue of Khons Neferhetep, and on the stele it is recorded that the god nodded twice to give his consent. Apparently the statue was rigged by the priests in such a manner as to permit the head to nod—at their command, of course—when the answer to the request was to be positive. When the answer was negative, the statue probably sat there, still as stone. On this occasion, the statue nodded its assent and was asked to transfer magical powers to a second statue which would then act as a god and travel to cure the girl. It was believed that a god could transfer his power to a statue that represented him, and the statue of Khons Neferhetep was probably equipped so that when a statue of Khons was brought near, the first statue—with priestly assistance—could lift an arm and give divine blessing to the second statue.

Assured of Khons Neferhetep's power, Khons left on the long trip to Bekhten. He went straight to the sick room where the princess suffered and soon used his magical powers to drive the evil spirit from her body: the girl arose cured. Moreover, the evil spirit was so impressed by Khons's powers, that he surrendered easily and volunteered to return to his own land without creating problems. He did ask before taking his leave, however, to sit with Khons at a feast given in their honor by the prince of Bekhten. This was arranged: god, demon, and prince spent a pleasant day in each other's company. Afterwards the demon went home as he had promised.

When the prince saw the power of Khons, he determined to keep the god in Bekhten as long as possible and did, in fact, persuade him to stay for three years, four months, and five days. Eventually the god became ready to return home and flew out of his shrine in the form of a golden hawk. The prince then sent back to Thebes Khons's chariot full of gifts for the Egyptians who had saved his daughter's life. These presents were taken to the temple and laid at the foot of Khons Neferhetep, who was thereafter worshipped as the god ''who could perform mighty deeds and miracles and vanquish the demons of darkness.''

The chief shrine for the worship of Khons was inside the complex of the Temple of Karnak. Ramesses III began the Temple of Khons there and it was finished by his successors. Its wall carvings show the various kings responsible for the temple as they worship Khons and his parents.

# 10

# Thoth and Maat:   Gods of the Intellect

Even though they were not related in a family or triad, Thoth and
Maat were often considered jointly, and together they provide us with
valuable insights into Egyptian mythology.  Both represented qualities
of the intellect—wisdom and truth; but there were major differences
in the ways the two were thought of.  Maat—truth and justice—was
not nearly as well developed mythologically (that is, as a character in
stories) as was Thoth—wisdom.   The former, a feminine
personification, was ethereal and abstract while the latter was
depicted in concrete and specific images.  The view of Maat was
philosophical and theoretical while the concept of Thoth was personal
and practical.  The contrasts, however,  should not be taken too far:
Thoth, however personal and visual his representation, did represent
an important intellectual concept; and Maat, however abstract her
qualities, was depicted as a concrete figure who was at times involved
in the myths of other gods.  Both god and goddess represented human
and divine qualities necessary for a satisfactory life and for passage
through the underworld.  They were placed as a pair in the solar boat
to set its course, providing guidance for Ra and his companions during
their passage through the sky.
    Even though they had important roles in the mythologies of
Memphis, Annu, and Thebes, Thoth and Maat were not normally
made close "blood" relatives of the divine families in those cities.
When the priests there created family trees for their gods, these two

were placed out on a limb. They did, though, play important supporting roles in the stories evolved at the major cult centers. Thoth, in particular, figured in many myths from the Delta to the far South and was called at one time "the mightiest of the gods," for reasons which we shall see. His own cult center, Hermopolis, was not dominant politically and this may explain why its mythology remained local and why Thoth never became chief god of all Egypt.

## The Doctrine of Creation at Hermopolis

In stories from around Egypt, we have uncovered numerous versions of the creation of the world and of the gods and humans who populate it, but one of the most unusual and interesting came from the unlikely village of Hermopolis, a town of no political importance. Thoth's cult center was in this small town in Middle Egypt near the present city of Minia. Priests there espoused a mythology at an early date, and evidence of its influence can be found in the Pyramid Texts. No surviving document or monument sets it out as a system; most references to Hermopolis occur in documents late enough to show influence from the more politically important religious centers. The outline of the original Hermopolitan mythology, nevertheless, can be discovered, and is now thought to be a mythical explanation of the ebbing of the Nile flood, which left behind it mounds of earth teeming with life.

While other versions of the creation tended to tell stories of distinct events involving gods with distinct characters, the view of creation at Hermopolis was more abstract, though not entirely so. This mythology described the work of four elements which arose from the chaos and gave shape to it. The elements were given names, but not the elaborate personalities of Ra, Ptah, and Atum, the major gods in other creation myths. Even the characteristics which the elements represented were abstract.

An early papyrus has preserved the celebration by an ancient poet of the first stages in this creation myth:

Salutations to you, you Five Great Gods,
Who come out of the City of Eight,

153

You who are not yet in heaven,
You who are not yet upon earth,
You who are not yet illuminated by the sun.

The poem tells how, on the Island of Flame, the primeval hill similar
to one on which Ra arose, the four gods came into being at the same
time; they were seen as some sort of force that existed between
heaven and earth. At first there were four elements and an unnamed
leader (the "Five Great Gods"), but once Thoth developed a national
role, he was thought of as leader and this became his creation story.
Each element brought with him his female component, giving the
total of eight elements. The group incuded Nun, the god of the
primeval ocean already seen in the mythology of Heliopolis, and his
consort Naunet; Heh, the god of the immeasurable, who with his
consort Heket was responsible for raising the sun; Kek, the god of
darkness, and his consort Keket gave the world the darkness of night
so that the sun would have a place to shine; and Amun, the god of
mystery, the hidden, and nothingness, who with his consort Amaunet
brought the air which breathed life into everything. The four males
were depicted as frogs and the females as serpents swimming around
in the mud and slime of chaos, the primeval nothingness from which
everything sprang. The Pyramid Texts said that "the Waters spoke to
Infinity, Nothingness, Nowhere, and Darkness"— meaning that Nun
spoke to his four male companions; and the creation began.
Eventually the eight elements came together and out of their union
came the primeval egg which could not be seen because it existed
before there was light. Out of the egg came the light of the sun which
the eight raised up into the sky.

## THOTH

Although the numerous irreconcilable accounts of Thoth's birth are
indicative of the lack of a systematic mythology for him, Siegfried
Morenz supports an account that associates him with Ra. An ancient
passage ascribes Thoth's birth to the powers of the chief sun god: "I
am Thoth, the eldest son of Ra, whom Atum has fashioned, created
from Khepri.... I descend to earth with the secrets of 'what belongs

to the horizon.' '' Since this version credited the birth not just to Ra alone, but to Atum and Khepri, other forms of Ra, Thoth was provided with a powerful trio of fathers; and it was significant that Thoth came into the world bearing powerful secrets.

While Thoth was viewed as the god of wisdom in general, he was known more specifically as the god of science and medicine, primarily because he was remembered for giving Isis the charms which brought Osiris back to life long enough to father Horus, and which later cured the sick Horus of his scorpion stings. He was also thought of as the source of rhetoric, names for objects, and the alphabet. He invented hieroglyphic writing, arithmetic, and astronomy. Despite these lofty attributes, Thoth could be one of the most amusingly and charmingly human of the gods. He was slow and garrulous when Isis needed him to cure Horus' stings. He was as confused as any of the other gods during the trial of Seth and Horus. On the other hand, he was fierce and bloody in the defense of any of the gods he thought wronged.

Much of Thoth's authority over men and gods came as a result of his being appointed deputy to Ra. We have seen that when Ra became tired of the burden of all his work, he delegated some of his duties to other gods and appointed Thoth his assistant: ''Inasmuch as I shall act so that the light may shine in the underworld... you shall be scribe there and keep in order those who reside there and those who may perform deeds of rebellion against me.... You shall be in my place, a place-taker. Thus you shall be called Thoth, the place-taker of Ra.'' Thoth was also the heart of Ra, which means that he was Ra's source of wisdom; and he had his place in the solar boat, where along with Maat, he set the course each day.

Ra gave Thoth the moon to balance Ra's own sun. As a moon god, Thoth used his knowledge of mathematics to measure the seasons and regulate time. He surveyed the heavens and planned the shape of the earth; it was his will that kept the earth and everything on it in equilibrium. The universe's stability depended on his knowledge of celestial mathematics. These attributes led him to be considered god of science.

The wide powers of Thoth involved him in numerous duties in behalf of both men and gods. The oldest surviving references to Thoth are found in the Pyramid Texts, in which he was assigned a role

155

in the underworld. He was to ferry the dead across the "winding waterway" on his wings. Once in the underworld on the other side of the water, he became a champion of the dead king and protected him from those that would do him harm. Later, many of the vignettes in the Book of the Dead gave him further underworld duties, standing beside the scales at the trial with a quill in hand to record the verdict on a papyrus scroll.

In another role Thoth was considered protector and messenger of the gods. He was expected to sharpen his knife and cut out the hearts and remove the heads of those who would do harm to god or king. His specific duty was to protect the Eye of Horus and see that it was conveyed to the king who sought immortality. Additionally, he was to protect justice and assure peace. The Pyramid Texts contain a prayer to him as peacemaker "Hear, O Thoth, in whom is the peace of the gods." One of the spells in the Coffin Texts claims he was the "Bull of Justice," even able to satisfy Horus and Seth, in whose struggles his role as peacemaker among the gods was most evident.

In order to fulfill these and other duties, Thoth invented the craft of writing, perhaps to the modern mind his most appealing contribution to learning. He kept written records of the seasons and celestial geometry; he was responsible for keeping the records of judgments on the dead and for writing letters on behalf of the gods at Annu. This function was described in the Book of the Dead: "I have brought the palette and the inkpot as being the objects which are in the hands of Thoth; hidden is that which is in them! Behold me in the character of a scribe." It is interesting that even his ability as a writer involved hidden knowledge, but Thoth's use of this art went far beyond performing secretarial services for the gods: he was also Annu's chief author. At times he was considered to be the author of the whole Book of the Dead, but more widely he was thought to have written only sections of it. One late papyrus claimed that Thoth wrote parts of the Book of Breathings "with his own fingers" and through this enabled souls to breathe for ever. His most ambitious writing project was called the Book of Thoth and contained his magic formulae, although the length of this book remains a matter of controversy. One version of the myth claimed only two pages for the book—one dealing with magic to charm nature, and the other giving the magic to control the world of the dead. Another version of the

Plate 45. Thoth as an ibis with writing tablet

myth claimed that were forty-two books dealing with law, the education of priests, the history of the world, geography, hieroglyphics, astronomy, astrology, religion, and medicine.

## The Book of Thoth

The Book of Thoth inspired one of the few stories about Thoth that does not involve some other god. A Ptolemaic papyrus tells of a prince named Neferkaptah, his family and their search for the Book of Thoth. A priest described the magical book to the prince in glowing terms:

> "Thoth wrote the book with his own hand, and in it was all the magic in the world. If you read the first page, you will enchant the sky, the earth, the abyss, the mountains, and the sea: you will understand the language of the birds of the air, and you will know what the creeping things of the earth are saying, and you will see the fishes from the darkest depths of the sea. And if you read the other page, even though you are dead and in the world of ghosts, you could come back to earth in the form you once had. And besides this, you will see the sun shining in the sky with the full moon and the stars, and you will behold the great shapes of the gods."

Naturally, the prince begged to be told where he could obtain the book, and after promising to provide his informant with an elaborate funeral he was told that the book was kept in the middle of the Nile near Koptos, locked in a series of valuable boxes. The prince ran to tell his wife Ahura this marvelous news, but she, fearful of the power of the gods, begged him not to search further. Undeterred by her warning, he set sail with his wife and son.

When they arrived in Koptos, they built a magical barge to search out the boxes on the river bed. After three days the crew found them, but when Neferkaptah used sand to build a coffer dam so that he could get to them, he discovered that they were guarded by great snakes, scorpions, and other crawling things which no man could kill. Neferkaptah, however, knew the magical spells to still these creatures, and walked through their midst unharmed. One by one he opened the boxes and soon arrived at the last, a golden one, where he found the Book of Thoth.

At once he used its wisdom to enchant nature—the fish came up from the bottom of the river for him to see—and he knew that the priest had spoken true. Calling for a sheet of papyrus and some beer, he wrote down the magical words of the book, then washed the ink off with beer. He drank the beer and so drank the words of Thoth and knew them. This done, he sailed for home with his small family.

When Thoth discovered the theft of his book, his anger was terrible. He used the powers of the gods to pull the son and wife of Neferkaptah from the boat and drown them. Grief-stricken, the prince used his own magic and raised the body of his wife to the surface, only to be told that in the underworld she had seen Thoth with his anger unabated. Now Neferkaptah knew that the god's magic was much stronger than his and that the end was inevitable. He wrapped the book to his chest with a fine piece of linen, for he was resolved that the god would never again have it; and shortly he too was pulled overboard to his death. The crew of the barge sailed on home and reported the sad news to the king, the prince's father, who put on mourning clothes and went looking for his son's body. He found it floating in the river with the book still bound to its chest. The prince was buried with the full honors due to the son of a king, and the Book of Thoth was buried with him. Thus was the vengeance of Thoth fulfilled but the book remained with Neferkaptah.

\*\*\*\*\*

Thoth normally appeared in one of two shapes: an ibis or a baboon. The baboon was probably the earlier representation of the two since at an early time the Egyptians revered the baboon and associated it with the sun god because of its chatterings at dawn. Apparently, the wisdom of the ape was associated with the god of wisdom. In this form Thoth was depicted as an ape with a dog-like face. The Temple of Ramesses II at Abu Simbel shows baboons worshipping the rising sun; giant apes stand at what used to be gates of a shrine to Thoth at El Ashuein not far from Minia: and more ape statues can be found in the Egyptian Museum. In vignettes for the

159

Book of the Dead this depiction of Thoth can be seen sitting on top of the scales in the trial, giving Thoth a double presence there since he also stood in his ibis form to record the verdict. This other depiction showed Thoth with a human body and an ibis head. The ibis was a long-beaked bird often seen in fields along the Nile, and according to one myth, when Ra made Thoth his deputy, he assigned him the ibis as a messenger to ease his burden. In either form, Thoth sometimes wore a lunar disk sitting in the crescent of a quarter moon, signifying his role as a moon god.

The contemporary traveler to Egypt will find remains of numerous places where Thoth was honored. In the Valley of the Kings he is seen as the ibis-headed god in many tombs, such as Seti I, and as a baboon in King Tutankhamun's tomb and elsewhere. Often in the temples of Upper Egypt he can be found in murals pouring libations over the heads of kings. The Egyptian Museum holds one of the more famous statues of Thoth as a baboon beside a scribe. Near Minia at Tounah el Gebel is the cemetery for ancient Hermopolis, including the tomb of Petosiris, a high priest of Thoth in Graeco-Roman times. This exquisite tomb with informative wall carvings contains a text which gives the creed by which the priest must have lived: "I will teach you as my god ordered me. I will take you to the right way in life. Everything that I did is the same as it is in the sacred book." Close by the tomb is one of the most macabre sites in Egypt, an elaborate underground necropolis possibly covering hundreds of acres in which sacred ibises and baboons were mummified and buried by the thousand as sacrifices to Thoth.

## MAAT

Maat was perhaps the least mythological of the Egyptian gods because she was the visual form given to a philosophical concept. Her physical form was a woman carrying the ankh and scepter, and she was most readily identified by the feather she wore on her head. No one knows for sure the origin of her association with the feather, usually described as an ostrich feather, but somehow the ethereal qualities of the feather seem well suited to a goddess of her characteristics. It has been suggested that the feather became her symbol because it is

equally behoved though because side of the ... weighing against the true
judgment required of ... and loosen tender ... to life ... in the trial of
the dead.

... The philosophical quality which the goddess represented was
thus called ... and sometimes translated as "truth", but to supply
a word will suffice to explain all that was implied by the concept.
Here was the key to the Egyptian view of ethical behaviour in human

Plate 46.  Thoth as both ibis and baboon

equally balanced along each side of the quill, suggesting the fine judgment required of a goddess who sat to judge truth in the trial of the dead.

The philosophical quality which the goddess represented was also called *maat* and our loose translation is "truth," but no single word will suffice to explain all that was indicated by the concept. *Maat* was the key to the Egyptian view of ethical behavior for humans while alive and of divine behavior in judging of souls after death. As Siegfried Morenz further explained: "Maat is right order in nature and society, as established by the act of creation, and hence means, according to the context, what is right, what is correct, law, order, justice, and truth." *Maat* was a guide to the correct attitude one should take to others.

In its simplest form *maat* was represented as an early hieroglyphic made up of intersecting straight lines which stood for the king's throne, suggesting that his decisions rested on *maat*.

The name probably translated originally as "that which is straight." The American romantic Ralph Waldo Emerson wrote in his nineteenth-century essay, "Nature," that one of the uses of nature is to provide metaphors for moral behavior. This is just what seems to have happened with *maat*. Straightness, which is a physical, geometric term, was perceived as symbolic of moral rectitude and then made visible in the hieroglyphic symbol used to indicate the concept. Straightness implies order, and the presence of *maat* stamped order on chaos at the moment of creation.

As Morenz suggests, when looking at ancient religions, one is always justified in asking if belief in the gods carried implications for human moral and ethical behavior. In Egyptian religion and politics the answer for the concept of *maat* was clearly yes; *maat* reflected an attitude that order in law was influenced by truth and justice, and that respect for order, truth, and justice was required of those in positions of authority. In later periods, Egyptian judges hearing a case were expected to carry the feather as a sign of their dedication to the eternal principles of the concept. An ancient text proclaims of *maat*: "Its good and its worth was to be lasting. It has not been disturbed since the day of its creation: whereas he who transgresses its ordinances is punished." *Maat*, then, represented, as E.A. Wallis

Plate 47.  Maat

Budge wrote, "the highest conception of physical and moral law and order known to the Egyptians."

It was to embody this concept that the goddess *Maat* was conceived. She was the personification of truth and justice, but she was given only minimal human characteristics. She was more of a metaphor for this important quality than a "flesh and blood" figure, as most other gods were. Her mythology says that she was supposed to have been the daughter of Ra and to have risen with him from the primeval waters at the moment of creation. In other words, the moral concepts Maat represented were as primordial as Ra and the waters from which he created himself; and throughout Egyptian mythology her father was associated with her in order to explain his fairness. In the Coffin Texts there was a brief, curious myth that brought the two together. Ra was old and tired and asked Nun for advice. Nun told the chief god that he should bring Maat close to him and kiss her in order to gain renewed life and vitality. It was the Book of the Dead which said that Maat and Thoth stood beside Horus in Ra's solar boat and set the course each day and that Ra "lives by Maat, the beautiful." Budge thought this meant that Ra "lives by unchanging and eternal law and order."

In her mythology Maat also played an important role in the underworld. During the trial of the deceased soul, Maat was always present. In some drawings her feather sat on top of the scales to guarantee fairness, and the heart of the deceased was always weighed on the balance against the feather. If the heart were found to balance perfectly with truth and justice—being neither too heavy nor too light for it—the dead person was judged to have passed the first test and to be nearing immortality. Then the deceased progressed to the Hall of Maat, or the Hall of Judgment, in which he had to give forty-two denials of sin and identify the magical names of the various parts of the door. Maat supervised these activities and, if the deceased completed these tasks correctly, she certified that the soul was ready for admittance into the presence of Osiris for final acceptance.

## The Blinding of Truth

Maat's abstract nature did not lead easily to detailed stories in which she had, as did other gods, a role suggestive of human behavior.

Her philosophical bearing had to be loftier than the common behavior of most gods. As a result she is often mentioned in myths, but she was not assigned major stories in which she was the central character. The lone exception proves the point. In the morality story of the conflict between Truth and Falsehood, the abstract qualities of Maat are prominent, but the character depicting them is male, not female. That a myth might use the different sex to depict Maat serves to demonstrate the abstract level at which the concept and the goddess were considered. The text, from about 1200 B.C., is badly damaged, but the story line is reasonably clear.

One day many years ago Truth borrowed a valuable knife from his brother, Falsehood, but as accidents will happen, he lost it. He explained the mishap to his brother and offered to replace it with another of equal quality. Falsehood had always been jealous of his brother and saw this as an opportunity to revenge years of imagined injuries. He refused the replacement and praised the missing knife: "Its blade came from the copper of the Mountain of El, its handle from the woods of Coptos, its scabbard from the tomb of the god, and its belt from the herds of Kal." Sensing he had the advantage, Falsehood pressed his claim before a court of nine gods. Truth had no choice but to confess he had lost the knife, and the court found in Falsehood's favor. For punishment, he insisted that Truth's eyes be blinded and that Truth be assigned to keep Falsehood's door.

So they lived for many days, but Truth's presence was a reminder to Falsehood of his own guilt. One day he called Truth's manservants aside and told them: "Abduct your lord and take him into the desert and cast him to the fierce lion who has many dangerous lionesses as mates, and they will devour him." The two men took their master and escorted him out of town, but on the way he pleaded with them, "Don't leave me to the lions in the desert. Give me bread and leave me in the hills where I may be found and cared for." Out of loyalty, the men did as he asked and returned to Falsehood to say that his orders had been carried out exactly and his brother was no more.

Truth wandered in the hills for several days, but one morning a lady, traveling away from home, passed him and was fascinated by his beauty, surpassing any man she had ever known. On returning home she sent her servant to bring the handsome man to her house to serve as doorkeeper. Once cleaned up, his beauty overpowered her and that evening she summoned him to her chambers. He spent hours in her bed and that night she became pregnant.

In due course she delivered a healthy son, who grew to be like no other boy in the land. In physical form he was more like a god than a mortal, and in scholarship he far excelled his schoolmates. Out of jealousy, however, they mocked him: "Whose son are you? You don't have a father."

So the boy went to his mother and asked about his father. She answered, "Do you see the blind doorkeeper? He is your father." Full of compassion, the boy took the man into his own chambers and sat him in a chair and placed a footstool under his feet. He brought food and drink and then begged the man to tell his story. When the boy heard how Falsehood had unfairly treated Truth and had him blinded without cause, he was scarcely able to contain his anger.

The boy set out to avenge his father's treatment. He took a wonderfully large ox of beautiful appearance, ten loaves of bread, a staff, and a sword. He traveled with his ox to Falsehood's land and approached Falsehood's herdsman. "I have traveled far and have far to go. Would you watch over my ox for me while I go to town?" When the herdsman asked what his pay would be, the boy gave him the bread, staff, and sword, and then disappeared.

Months went by, and one day Falsehood visited his fields. When he saw the magnificent ox, he told the herdsmen to prepare it for Falsehood's table. The man objected and told his master that the ox was not his to kill. Falsehood replied, "See, all the rest of my cattle are for you to use. Give one of them to the owner." So it was done as he commanded.

As soon as the boy heard, he came and demanded, "Where is my ox? I can't see it among your herd." The herdsmen told him he could take any of Falsehood's cattle as replacement, but the trap was sprung. He, of course, refused and demanded that Falsehood be tried before the same court of gods which had sentenced his father. In front of the court the boy claimed that there was no ox as wonderful as his, "Is there any ox as large as mine? If it should stand on the Island of Amun, the tip of its tail would lie upon the Papyrus Marshes, while its horns would stretch between the Eastern and Western Mountains, the Great River would be its spot for a bath, and it would give birth to sixty calves every day."

The court heard the testimony and accused the boy: "What you say is false. We have never seen so large an ox."

Then the boy had his victim. He asked the court, "Is there a knife with a copper blade from the mountain of El, wooden handle from Coptos, scabbard from the god's tomb, and belt from the herds of Kal?" The boy accused Falsehood, "Judge between Truth and Falsehood. I am Truth's son and have come to avenge his wrong."

Falsehood was quick to deny wronging his brother: "By Amun and by the king, if Truth be found alive, I should be blinded in both eyes and set as doorkeeper at his house."

The boy immediately produced his father and the court saw the truth in what he said. Falsehood was sentenced to the most severe punishment, given one hundred blows and five open wounds, blinded in both eyes, and set as doorman at Truth's house.

And so the boy avenged his father and Truth triumphed over Falsehood.

*****

Many of the vignettes in the Book of the Dead show Maat's important role during the trial of the dead, but there are other places that still today contain depictions of her. From Abu Simbel to the Valley of the Kings, she can be found in wall paintings and carvings; she is easily identified by the feather, usually on her head but sometimes held in her hand. She may also be found in the Egyptian Museum in numerous forms and depictions.

# 11

# Anubis

Primarily "Lord of the Mummy Wrapping," Anubis was one of the very old gods. He was depicted in the form of a dog or jackal, either as a man with a jackal head or as the full animal. Most likely the jackal was associated with death because he had been observed eating corpses, but Flinders Petrie speculated that the animals assembled in graveyards to feed off the offerings left there to honor the dead. A possible explanation for the cult of Anubis is that rituals in honor of the jackal were an attempt to put a benevolent interpretation on his practice of digging for bones in graveyards. In other words, if these macabre habits could be enshrined in mythology and religion, perhaps Anubis would use them for good rather than evil. Hence Anubis was given an important role in myths, especially in the underworld where he became responsible for caring for the bodies of the recently dead.

The earliest myths made Anubis the son of Ra, but the chief stories of Anubis gave him an altogether different genealogy, in which he had a clearly benevolent role. By the time of the Coffin Texts he was fully involved in the myths of Osiris. He was Nephthys' son, supposedly by her husband Seth; but in fact the child of her liaison with Osiris. The mother deserted her son in fear of Seth, but Isis found the child and raised him because he was the son of her now dead husband. Anubis became Isis' faithful watchdog and protector and was rewarded with the ability to understand human speech and to study medicine and the art of embalming.

Plate 48. Anubis

Following Osiris' death, Anubis was asked by Ra to assist Isis in reassembling the dismembered body. He and Horus, with Thoth's advice and magic, were able to wrap the body in mummy's cloth and restore it to its original shape. When he had finished his work, Anubis said to his father: "Arise and live: Behold your new appearance. Avert the crime of him who did you wrong." This act made Anubis valuable to human beings who hoped that he would do the same for their bodies when the time came.

As a result, he was assigned major roles in the afterlife in the Book of the Dead and elsewhere. Known as "Counter of Hearts," he greeted the dead on their entrance into the underworld and worked along with Horus to embalm the bodies and preserve the mortal remains from decay. He presided over "God's Booth" which contained four jars holding the necessary ingredients to deify the dead king. Then he was shown as the weigher of hearts during the trial, and it was his hand that checked the balance beam to determine the results. Souls which failed to pass were devoured by Ammit, one of the more fantastic of mythological creatures. At the trial he stood near Anubis, eager for the tasty dish that was his should the soul fail the test. He was a composite of three ferocious animals: he had the head of a crocodile, the body of a lion, and the backside of a hippopotamus; his name meant "eater of the dead."

Sometimes Anubis was thought of as the god who led the dead into the presence of Osiris for final judgment, although Horus also often had that assignment. Anubis was also shown supporting the upright mummy during the episode of the Opening of the Mouth. To symbolize the importance of this myth, during the actual embalming of the body a priest wore a jackal mask to indicate that he was Anubis' representative in this ritual.

By the twenty-first dynasty Anubis had become a generally popular god. The papyrus of Nisti-Ta-Nebet-Taui called him "Lord of the Holy Land" and claimed that "he gives gifts and food, all good and pure things, all things beautiful and sweet which the heaven gives, which are found on earth, which are brought by the Nile from his cave for Osiris." Later still, Anubis remained an important god for the Greeks and Romans. Plutarch reported that he was the one who connected the visible with the invisible world.

**Plate 49. Ammit**

# The Tale of the Two Brothers

Anubis was a central figure in one of the most elaborate Egyptian stories to have survived. "The Tale of the Two Brothers" is a complex narrative combining elements of myths and folktales into a delightful and human story. The chief characters are Anubis and Bata, a lesser known god of considerable antiquity from Sako in Middle Egypt. In the tale the two are depicted at first, more as humans than as gods, but later there are supernatural events which demonstrate the two have more than mortal powers. The tale has been variously interpreted as portraying a conflict between the two gods which ended in happy reconciliation or as describing the conflict between neighboring villages, though these need not be conflicting interpretations. Anubis has the lesser role of the two gods and only in his efforts to restore his brother to life does his part here reflect his traditional characterization, but this well-known tale provides important insights into Egyptian myth and folklore.

Once many years ago there were two brothers; the elder was Anubis and his younger brother was Bata. Anubis lived in his own home with his comely wife and Bata farmed for him. Bata tended the crops and animals and greatly increased Anubis' wealth, for he had the power of a god within him. Each day Bata worked in the fields, then reported to his elder brother of his labor. Each evening Bata retired to his own bed in the stable where he watched over the cattle.

In the mornings as he drove the cattle to the fields, he talked with them and asked where the best grazing would be that day. They would reply, "The grazing will be good today in such and such a field." With such care the cattle flourished and multiplied.

When the season for planting the fields came, Anubis told his brother, "In the morning have ready a yoke of oxen to plow the earth and seed to plant in the new turned land." At dawn the two brothers set forth for the field and worked side by side with vigor and friendship. When they had planted their supply of seed, Anubis sent his brother back to the house to fetch more.

Approaching the house, Bata saw his sister-in-law combing and plaiting her hair. "Go quickly," he said, "and bring me seed that I may hurry back to the fields." But she was no help: "Go yourself and open the bins because I am busy with my own work." Bata did as he was told, and soon burdened his shoulders with a heavy vessel of barley and emmer. When the wife saw his muscles strain with the heavy load, she became aroused and called out to Bata, "Come and stay with me an hour and we will take our pleasures. I will make it to your advantage and stitch fine clothes for you as a reward."

Bata was furious at the proposal and immediately rejected her. "You have been to me as a mother and what you suggest is an abomination. Say no more about it and I will keep quiet and tell no one myself." With this rebuke he took his seed and hastened to the fields, where he kept all this to himself.

Nevertheless, that evening as Anubis returned from his labors, leaving Bata to bring in the cows and equipment, the wife decided she had better be prepared to protect herself. She made it look as though she had been beaten and took a drug to make her vomit. When Anubis entered the house and saw his wife in cruel condition, he asked who had offended her. "No one has come near me but your brother," she confessed. "When he came to get the seed, he saw me and asked me to lie with him. When I refused, he beat me."

At this story, the elder brother became as angry as a leopard and took his spear and hid behind the door of the stable to attack Bata when he entered. When Bata approached the building, the first cow he was driving warned him, "Take care. Your brother is waiting to ambush you." The second cow repeated the caution. When Bata looked under the crack of the stable door, he saw Anubis' feet and quickly ran away, with his brother in close chase.

Bata called to Ra-Herakhty, "My great god, you are he who judges between the right and the wrong. Save me from this evil I do not understand." Ra heard his prayer and caused a great body of water full of crocodiles to spring between the brothers, and Anubis could not get at his brother. Even at the next dawn Bata was safe from all Anubis wanted to do to him. Bata called across the water, "Why do you want to harm me? It was your wife who tried to seduce me and I am innocent. Do you take the word of a whore over mine?" With that, Bata took a reed knife and cut off his own penis and threw it into the water, where the fish ate it. Bata then told his brother that he was leaving the land and journeying to the Valley of the Cedars (Lebanon?): "There I will take out my heart and place it high in the cedar on a flower. If the tree is cut down, I will appear to die, but if you spend seven years seeking the tree and find it and place my heart like a seed in water, I will live again. You will know you are needed when you find your pot of beer in a froth."

With that, Bata went away to the Valley of Cedar and Anubis entered his house full of grief. He slew his wife and cast her to the dogs and mourned his brother.

After a long journey, Bata found a tall cedar and placed his heart on top of its flower in the highest branches. He built a fine house for himself and he lived in contentment, except that he lacked a wife.

One day he met with the Nine Gods who told him that Anubis now understood the truth and had slain his false wife. Ra-Herakhty asked Khnum to make a wife to keep Bata company, and the god fashioned a woman on his potter's wheel. She was the fairest woman in the land and had the essence of all the gods in her. But the Seven Hathors came like the fates and foretold that she would die a violent death.

Bata loved his wife and laid before her all the game he killed. He cautioned her not to leave the house: "Go you not out for fear the sea will carry you away. As I am no longer a complete man, I cannot protect you." He told her about his heart in the top of the cedar.

One day while he was hunting, his wife disobeyed orders and wandered out alone. When the sea saw and chased her, she ran toward the security of her home. The sea asked the cedar to catch her, but all the tree could do was snip a lock of her hair. Accepting the hair, the sea carried it on its waves to Egypt and deposited it on the shore where the women were washing the king's clothes. The hair perfumed the wash and left a wonderfully sweet smell in the garments. The king consulted with his wisest advisors in order to discover the source of the perfume. One of their number told the king, "This lock of hair belongs to a daughter of Ra-Herakhty and she is made of the essence of all the gods." The king then sent his men into all the lands searching for the woman, and not without difficulty they found her and brought her to him. He immediately fell in love with the beautiful woman, and she told him of her husband and his heart in the tree. The king gave orders, "Have the tree cut down and the flower destroyed." And his men found the tree and cut off its flower, and in that instant Bata died.

Shortly afterward, Anubis sat down to a meal. When his beer

174

Plate 50.   **Anubis**

was placed in front of him it had fermented and produced froth and he knew this omen was a message for him. At once he set on his journey to the Valley of Cedars; there he found his brother's body lying dead in his house and he went in search of the heart. For three years he sought it in vain and one day said to himself that this was his last night on the quest as he longed to return to Egypt. He spent the next day in search and at dusk gave up. He had found only the berry from the cedar and as a memento took it home. Unknown to him, this was the heart he had so long sought. At home he sat down and dropped the berry in a cup of cold water. Overnight the berry soaked up the water and began to thrive. Bata's body, which had been brought along on the quest, began to shudder and he opened his eyes while the heart was still in the cup. Anubis took the cup and gave it to his younger brother to drink. When he swallowed the liquid and its contents, the heart returned to its rightful place and Bata was well again. The brothers embraced and Bata knew Anubis' devotion in search of his heart.

Bata then said to his elder brother, "I will take the form of a great bull with special markings and you will ride on my back. We will go together to my wife and the king and you will be richly rewarded for bringing so fine an ox to the king."

At dawn Anubis and Bata journeyed to the king. The entire land rejoiced at the sight of so marvelous an animal; they gave him his weight in gold and silver and he returned to his village to live.

One day soon after, the bull entered the kitchen at the palace and found the wife, who was now favored by the king. Suddenly he said aloud, "Look, it's me. I am alive." She replied, "Who are you?" — " I am Bata. You knew when you asked that the tree be cut down, I would die. But here I am. See, I am alive and am a bull."

This did not please the woman, who went to the king and coquettishly begged for a favor using all her womanly charms. "Let me eat the liver of this bull for he is not worth anything." The king regretted the death of so fine a bull, but he yielded in order to keep his new consort happy. A great festival was proclaimed and the bull was slaughtered as sacrifice. At the moment of death, the bull shook himself and caused two drops of blood to fall beside the door of the king's palace. In an instant two great persea trees grew where the blood had landed, and all the land rejoiced at so marvelous a sight.

When the king and his consort came to witness the trees, Bata, who was living in the heart of the tree, secretly told his wife, "See, I'm still alive. I am Bata and you have tried to kill me twice." Again the woman worked her way with the king: "Cut down the persea trees and have them made into fine furniture for your house." The king could not resist so comely a woman and did as she requested. The finest craftsman in the nation was sent for. As he felled the trees and began to mill them, a chip from the tree flew from his ax and entered the mouth of the king's consort, who became pregnant. In due time she delivered a handsome boy who was said to be the son of the king. The entire land rejoiced and the king appointed the child Viceroy of Kush and later Crown Prince of the whole country.

The king ruled for many more years, but eventually he flew into heaven. His son, as new king, called his royal counsellors into session and told them that he and Bata were one and the same. He then accused his wife (and mother) and bore testimony of her wickedness. The counsellors agreed with Bata in his harsh sentence on the disgraced woman. The new king then summoned Anubis to his side and appointed him crown prince. Bata ruled for thirty years and at his death his elder brother acceded to the throne.

\*\*\*\*\*

For the modern visitor to Egypt, Anubis is one of the most visible of the gods. There are numerous drawings of him in various papyri, especially in the vignettes of the Book of the Dead, and on the walls of tombs and temples from Abydos to Aswan. Probably his most graceful representation is the statue of a reclining but alert black animal in the Tutankhamun collection in the Egyptian Museum.

# 12

# Three Additional Fertility Gods: Hapi, Khnum, and Min

Mythologies from most ancient cultures were often concerned with nature's renewal, from the daily reappearance of the sun, to the coming of spring or the flood, to the replacement of the king at his death, to the achievement of the afterlife. The continuation of life was of great importance to early man and the mysteries of renewal became the catalysts of many basic myths. Egyptian mythology was rich in gods and myths associated with renewal, and the various forms of the sun god, the survival of Osiris, the concepts of kingship were all manifestations of it. Three additional gods were closely connected with fertility, and each in his own way illustrated some aspects of rejuvenation.

## HAPI

From the border south of Abu Simbel, through the cataracts near Aswan, north toward Cairo and the sea, the river Nile flows through Egypt for over a thousand miles. The river has brought life to the desert and created a thin strip of green that provides water and food to millions of Egyptians and their animals. The source of all Egyptian life, the Nile was also the source of great mystery: Where did it begin? What made it flood each year? What determined how high and waters would used ... it is not impossible, therefore, that the great and mysterious river should be the source of underworld Egypt. Through about the beginning, it works his along the river, his impulse role for it in his religion and his mythology, that role took its most concrete form in the personification of the river into the god Hapi ...

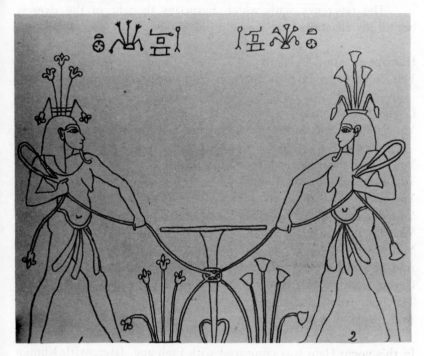

**Plate 51.   Hapi as god of the south Nile (left) and north Nile (right)**

the waters would rise? It is not surprising, therefore, that this great and mysterious river would be the source of much mythology. From almost the beginning of man's life along the river, he found a role for it in his religion and his mythology; that role took its most concrete form in the personification of the river into the god Hapi.

The reverence with which Egyptians thought of the river is beautifully illustrated in a lovely old hymn:

Homage to you, O Hapi!
You come forth in this land and come in peace to make Egypt live,
O you hidden one,
You guide of the darkness whensoever it is your pleasure to be its guide.
You water the fields which Ra has created,
You make all animals live,
You make the land drink without ceasing;
You descend the path of heaven,
You are the friend of meat and drink;
You are the giver of the grain,
And you make every place of work flourish, O Ptah!...
If you were to be overcome in heaven,
The gods would fall down headlong,
And mankind would perish.

In this poem Hapi was compared with Ptah and, later, with Khnum because the poet thought of all three as creation gods who brought life to the earth. Since both men and the land receive nourishment for life from the river, Hapi was said to be so important that if he were somehow to fail, all the gods would fall from heaven and all men would die.

Hapi was thought to live in a cavern in the region of the first cataract from which the waters flowed, and the annual flood was called "the arrival of Hapi." The god was depicted as a man with long hair and the heavy breasts of an old woman. This androgynous form combined the male and female life-producing forces. Actually there was a Hapi of the southern river and another for the northern river. The one from the south wore a headpiece of a clump of lotus flowers; the northern one wore papyrus flowers. When the two were depicted as a single god, he would carry both flowers as a sign of the union of Upper and Lower Egypt and is often seen in wall carvings knotting them together.

Because Hapi was the Nile and the river brought food, many other gods were associated with him. A hymn to Ra claimed that the sun god created the river, supposedly at the same time as he gave shape to the watery abyss. In the Coffin Texts Hapi referred to himself as "the Primeval One of the earth." This text made Hapi coeval with Nun, the watery abyss that existed at the beginning: and early in Egyptian mythology Hapi assumed the attributes of Nun. In addition, the story of Osiris connects the river to the great god of vegetation. It was on the waters of Hapi that Osiris floated until Isis found the pieces and took them to be reunited.

Primarily, Hapi was thought of as the source of food. In the Pyramid Texts he was to provide the food King Unas needed in the next life. There is also a prayer to the god of the river asking him to provide the grains that will nourish the king.

By the time of the Coffin Texts the concept of Hapi had been more fully developed. There was a spell intended to assist the recently dead soul in attaining the attributes of Hapi:

I am the Nile God, the lord of provisions,
Who comes with joy, the well beloved....
I am the Great One who protects the gods regarding their cakes, the
    Primeval One of Earth....
I am the Nile God, the lord of waters,
Who brings vegetation,
And I will not be driven off by my enemies....
I have come that I may make the Two Lands green....

In the Book of the Dead a soul prayed that he might gain the power of Hapi. It was his wish to drink from the waters of the canal in order to gain power over the green plants and herbs and bring gifts to the gods.

# KHNUM

The chief god in the mythology of Elephantine Island in the Nile at Aswan was Khnum, who headed his own triad. He was the god of the cataract region, which included the sources of the Nile guarded by Hapi. There is evidence in the Pyramid Texts that he had been known long before the time of those writings, but no one knows for sure just how long he had been worshipped. Apparently he came to be known as a creator god rather late, but he survived until two or three centuries after Christ. He was represented on monuments as a man with a ram's head, holding a scepter and ankh. Often the white crown of Upper Egypt was on his head, and sometimes the crown was decorated with plumes, a disk, or cobras. Occasionally a jug of water, representing the Nile, rested over his ram's horns.

Like most chief gods, he was later considered a creator. His followers thought that on his potter's wheel he molded an egg from which sprang the sun. Wall-carvings at various temples in the Luxor area show him sitting at his potter's wheel on which he is fashioning a child; he was thought of as the master craftsman who molded a child out of clay and then implanted him as a seed in his mother's womb. In this manner he was considered the "father of fathers and the mother of mothers." It was said he created the gods in a similar manner.

Khnum was thought to be the combination of the forces that made up the entire world; he was Ra, the sun; Shu, the air: Osiris, the underworld; and Geb, the earth—all wrapped up in one figure. In this form he was represented as a man with four ram's heads.

A Ptolemaic inscription preserves for us an interesting myth about Khnum's role in a seven-year drought that must have been an old story when it was finally written down. The story supposedly took place during the reign of a king of the third dynasty, possibly Zoser, who became increasingly concerned about the drought that plagued his country year after year without relief. For seven years the Nile had failed to rise enough to flood sufficient land to grow the needed crops, and so the king sent a message to the governor of the south, inquiring about the source of the Nile. On being told that its waters came from a double cavern which was compared to twin breasts, the source of all good things, the king decided to visit the Nile god who watched over the river and emerged at the time of the

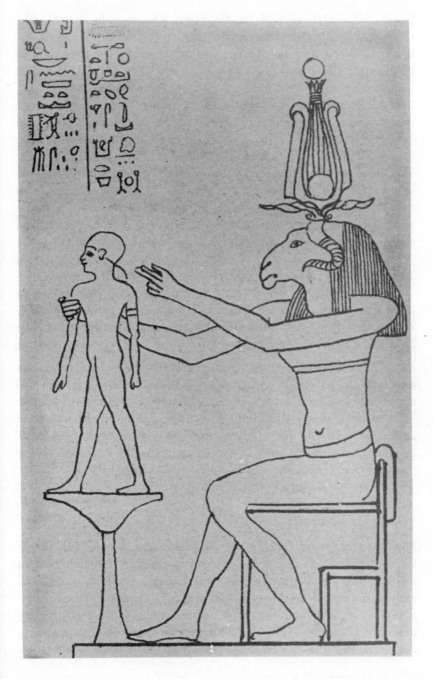

Plate 52. Khnum fashioning man on his potter's wheel

flood. The gatekeeper of the flood was Khnum, who guarded the doors which kept the waters in and then, at the right moment, threw open the doors to let the floods loose on the land. The king went to Elephantine Island and made proper sacrifices to Khnum who then appeared in front of the royal visitor from the north: "I am Khnum," he said, "the Creator. My hands rest upon you to protect your person and to make your body sound. I gave you your heart.... . I am he who rises at his will to give health to those who toil. I am the guide and director of all men, the Almighty, the father of the gods, Shu, the mighty possessor of the earth." The god went on to complain that no one took care to keep his shrine in good repair even though there were plenty of stones in the neighborhood to use in the work. The king promised that this wrong would be corrected, and the god promised in return that the Nile would once again rise every year as it had in the old days. The king ordered a tax to be levied anually on local produce and the proceeds applied to the maintenance of a priesthood for Khnum (dare we now speculate that the entire myth was made up by a latter=day king and priests, who conspired to raise a tax and needed justification?). It must be assumed that both king and god kept their promises.

The triad of Elephantine was completed by two goddesses associated with fertility. Satis was Khnum's consort, giver of the waters used in the rituals of purification of the dead. Called "dispenser of cool water coming from Elephantine," she was later associated with Isis and Hathor. Her sister Anuket was the third member of the triad. The name of this human-shaped goddess meant "to embrace," and she was possibly the goddess of lust.

## MIN

Min was the god of fertility and was celebrated in one of the more interesting festivals during the twentieth dynasty. His cult centers were Koptos and Panopolis, and there is evidence of his worship as early as the first dynasty, perhaps even earlier. Eventually he became a vegetation god, and one brief myth from the eleventh dynasty described his curious activity of bringing rain to the desert; apparently during the rainstorm he became visible to mortals. Both as vegetation

Plate 53. Min: the physical alteration was made by the nineteenth-century editor.

god and as bringer of rain to barren land, he was fulfilling his duties as god of fertility.

The usual depiction of Min presented him with the necessary attributes for a fertility god. He was drawn in human form standing with his feet close together and his penis erect. He holds an arm above his head and in his hand is a flail. His headpiece was usually the two plumes of Amun, and he had two streamers hanging down the back of his neck. Many of the chief gods were associated with Min in order to demonstrate that they had his virility; at one time or another Ptah, Amun-Ra, Khons, and Horus were represented as Min. The association with Horus also meant that the kings, who assumed the identity of Horus while they lived, attained the sexual vitality of Min.

Pre-literate societies depended heavily on the health and strength of their kings. If a king were sickly or weak, he could not lead his people in battle and might not be able to produce an heir, thereby causing strife over his succession. As a result these societies devised numerous tests of the health and strength of their kings, most of which revolved around the periodic renewal of the king's physical powers. On the plain before Luxor is the Temple of Medient Habu, the mortuary temple of Ramesses III, built during the twentieth dynasty. The walls of this temple contain carvings of the annual festival of Min at harvest time, during which the kings renewed their powers and were "reborn" with increased vigor. In the opening scene the king went to the "house of his father Min," the local temple, accompanied by his sons, priests, musicians, and guards. There he worshiped the god and poured libations in his honor. Min in this episode was addressed as Amun-Ra-Khamutef, a combination of sun and moon gods.

In the next scene the god was carried out of his sanctuary by twenty priests, and a short procession, including the king, queen, a white bull, priests, and others, carried the statue on poles to a nearby festival site. Some of the priests carried a box of lettuce leaves, which were credited with aphrodisiac powers. (The explanation for this use of the lettuce plant remains obscure, although we have seen another example of it during the satirical version of the fight between Seth and Horus.). The group proceeded to the "Stairs of Min," a platform with steps on which the statue was placed. The statue, according to the text, then caused the king to make great sacrifices. What happened next was supposed to represent the symbolic death and rebirth of the king/god, which in turn suggested the death and rebirth of the land whose virility was thought to be connected with the king's. The services began with the singing of hymns of praise; then the king cut a sheaf of wheat with a sickle, symbolizing the death of the wheat at the moment of harvest. During this act, the queen, as the personification of Isis, walked around her husband and uttered a spell, probably intended to assure his rebirth. The next act was the sacrifice of the bull which apparently served as surrogate for the king. The dead bull's ear was severed and presented to the king as a reminder that he too was mortal, and the bull's tail was cut off and shown to the assembled people. The king paraded around the stairs and eventually embraced the queen in the form of Isis while the people chanted hymns. The embrace was symbolic of the rebirth of the king as Min, and he was restored to purity, fertility, and vitality. Four birds were released to carry the good news to the four points of the compass, and the king offered the first fruits of the harvest to Min, whose statue was returned to his temple. It is possible that the rituals of the Sacred Marriage were celebrated between the king as Min and his wife as Isis or Hathor toward the end of the festival, but the sources of information are damaged at this point and the exact details are impossible to determine.

This festival celebrated Min as the god of fertility, which was his most prominent role; but Eva R. Meyerowitz, in a work on the rituals associated with the divine kingship in Egypt which includes an elaborate explanation of the festival just described, claims that Min was also given other duties. He was associated with the moon and considered a storm god illuminated by meteorites and thunderbolts. His statue was painted black to represent a stormy night.

# 13

# Postscript

Like all myths, those of Egypt had (and still have) universal qualities that address and satisfy human needs, such as the need for models of rites of passage, heroic behavior, or family structure. Myths are methods of explaining the human desire for love, justice, honor, learning, and other universals.

Like many myths, these told mortals what they needed to know about survival in complex situations. Myths provided conventions and rituals of worship, politics, marriage, and sex which assist us in dealing with life. Moreover, they touched on and explained essential components of nature—the sun, moon, water, vegetation, storms, floods, eclipses. They explained nature's origins and its continuing importance and gave meaning to natural phenomena that otherwise seemed eccentric, capricious, or accidental.

As Joseph Campbell has written in *Flight of the Wild Gander*, "Mythology is the picture language of metaphysics"; Egyptian myths dealt with the abstract as well as the practical and helped explain the metaphysical aspects of life. Maat and Thoth, for example, were statements of elevated thinking and behavior considered essential for a full life. Egyptian mythology also embraced the apparent dualities and ambiguities that are part of life: good and evil, ruler and ruled, night and day, feast and famine. Seth, for example was to be both feared and admired, both defeated and used. Like many products of man's fantasy, Egyptian mythology gave assurances of immortality and provided detailed information on the next life as well as guidance to those seeking immortality.

According to Plutarch, during one of the annual Egyptian festivals, the people repeated the words, "Truth is sweet," while eating figs and honey. Ananda K. Coomaraswamy has explained that truth is the key element in mythology: "Myth is the penultimate truth, of which all experience is the temporal reflection. The mythical narrative is of timeless and placeless validity, true now, ever and everywhere." Somewhere in Egyptian mythology lies truth that provides us clues into the workings of ancient Egyptian minds and into our own timeless questing.

Basically, however, these myths were and remain good stories which provided entertainment during festivals, amusement around campfires, and subject matter for artists of all sorts.

Professor George Gerbner has reminded us that "man is an animal who lives in, of, and by his fantasies. He is a storytelling animal." Some of these stories become myths which express the truth about life, death, and life after death. One of Plato's characters, an Egyptian, told his Greek audience: "There is nothing beautiful or great nor remarkable done, be it in your country, or here, or in another country known to us, which has not long since been consigned to writing and preserved in our temples." The myths of beautiful, great, and remarkable deeds and thoughts—long preserved in temples and elswhere—have here been retold in an effort to better understand man as a storytelling animal seeking the truth about himself and his ancestors.

# Checklist of Characters
# From Egyptian Mythology

### by
### Alison Baker

Variant names and spellings are given for the major figures in this book.

AKER: As guardian of the gates of dawn through which the sun passed each morning, Aker was represented in the form of a lion and was an earth god. (See *Dua* and *Sef*.)

AMAUNET: Consort of Amun, she was represented with a serpent's head.

AMMIT: This monster—part hippopotamus, lion, and crocodile—sat under the scale next to Anubis at the judgment of the dead.

AMUN (Amen, Amon): God of the wind and of the breath of life, Amun was the local god of Thebes. Usually represented as a man wearing a high crown with two plumes and holding a sceptre and ankh, he became during the Middle Kingdom a national deity as the composite god, Amun-Ra.

ANEDJTI: Originally chief deity of Busiris, he was represented as a king, holding a crooked sceptre and flail and wearing two feathers on his head; later associated with Osiris.

ANTHAT: Syrian war goddess adopted by the Egyptians during their Asiatic conquests, she was depicted seated, holding a club, spear, and shield, or standing, holding the ankh.

ANUBIS (Anpu): God of mummification and inventor of funeral rites, he was represented either with the body of a man and head of a jackal or as a jackal lying on a shrine; worshipped primarily at Asiut.

ANUKIS: Regional goddess of the first cataract at Aswan, she was the wife of Khnum and mother of Satis. She was depicted with negroid features and wore a tall feather plume.

APIS: Sacred bull at Memphis, Apis was black with a triangular spot of white on his forehead, various markings on his body, and after the New Kingdom a solar disk on his forehead. He was buried in the great Serapeum at Sakkara.

APOPHIS (Apep): During the journeys of gods and men through the underworld and the night, the evil serpent Apophis led hordes of monsters in attacks against the travelers.

ASTARTE: Syrian war goddess mentioned in the Bible and adopted by the Egyptians, she was associated with the moon and Hathor. She was depicted riding a horse naked, wearing only the white crown with two plumes.

ATEN: Represented as the solar disk with long rays terminating in hands holding ankhs, he was promoted to sole deity under the religious reforms of Amenhetep IV, who changed his name to Akenaten and moved his capital to Tel el-Amarna

ATUM (Temu, Tem, Atem): Local god of Heliopolis and later regarded as an aspect of the sun god Ra, Atum was believed to have fathered the human race and all living forms. He was depicted in human form, usually wearing the double crown of Upper and Lower Egypt.

BAEL: Asiatic god adopted by the Egyptians, he was associated with Seth as god of war and with the destructive forces of the sky: blazing heat and stormy winds.

BASTET: Cat-headed goddess worshipped at Bubastis, she became a goddess of pleasure and a protective deity against evil spirits. Still later she was worshipped in the form of sacred cats, often mummified and buried.

BES: Stout, full-faced dwarf with a curly beard, he was associated with birth and the household; as god of dance, music, and pleasure, he was responsible for the amusement of children.

BUCHIS: Montu's sacred bull at Hermonthis and thought to be an incarnation of Ra or Osiris, Buchis bulls were buried in underground vaults.

DUA: One of two protective lions guarding the passage through which the sun passed every morning, Dua ("tomorrow") and his partner Sef may be later forms of the lion Aker.

DUAMUTEF: Jackal-headed son of Horus, he was found on the canopic jar containing the stomach removed from the corpse before mummification. Associated with the east point of the compass, he and his brothers also appeared on a lotus flower before Osiris in the judgment scene.

GEB (Seb, Keb): God of the earth, Geb and his sister Nut were the second generation in the Great Ennead of Heliopolis; he was usually depicted as a man wearing the crown of lower Egypt.

HAPI (Hapy, Hap): Fertility god of the Nile, Hapi was depicted as a long-haired man with female breasts and a massive belly. He was especially worshipped at Elephantine and Gebel Silsileh.

HAPY: Ape-headed son of Horus, he was found on the canopic jar containing the lungs removed from the corpse before mummification. Associated with the northern cardinal point, he and his brothers also appeared on a lotus flower before Osiris in the judgment scene.

HATHOR: Originally a sky goddess, she became protector of women and a goddess of pleasure and was represented as a cow or as a woman wearing a solar disk between cow horns on her head. Her cult center was at Dendera.

HEH: This god's name literally meant 'a million' and signified the endless years of eternity; he was usually depicted kneeling and holding a notched reed.

HEKET: Frog-headed goddess associated with life, she presided at births as mid-wife. Her special places of worship were the town of Her-Wer and the Temple of Hatshepsut.

HERAKHYT: God of the sun's daily passage from the eastern to the western horizon, this falcon-headed god was worshipped at Edfu and was seen as a form of Horus.

HERSHEF: God of the Nile whose principle sanctuary was in the Fayum, he was represented as a ram-headed man, wearing on his head the white crown with plumes, a solar disk, lunar disk, and two serpents with disks on their heads.

HORUS: The filial piety expressed in his pursuit of Seth to avenge his father Osiris' murder was the most popular aspect of this god's myths. Represented as a falcon or as a man with a falcon head, he was originally god of the sky; but there were as many as twenty different Horuses in the Egyptian pantheon. His main cult centers were Edfu, Kom Ombo, and Heliopolis.

IHY: Son of Hathor and probably Horus of Edfu, he was represented as an infant playing the sistrum.

IMHOTEP (Imhetep, Iemhetep): Chief architect and vizier of King Zoser, who built the Step Pyramid at Sakkara, he was later deified and considered a son of Ptah at Memphis where he was worshipped as god of medicine. He was represented seated, with shaved head, reading a scroll.

IMSETY: Human-headed son of Horus, he was found on the canopic jar containing the liver removed from the corpse before mummification. Associated with the southern point of the compass, he and his brothers also appeared on a lotus flower before Osiris in the judgment scene.

ISAASET: Sometimes considered the female aspect of the bisexual god Atum, she was at Memphis the wife of Atum. She was depicted wearing a vulture headdress and holding the scepter and ankh.

ISIS: This goddess embodied the qualities of wifely fidelity and maternal feelings. Wife of Osiris and mother of Horus, she was known for her magical powers. She was usually depicted with cow's horns and solar disk on her head or with a throne as a headpiece.

KEK: One of the four male deities at Hermopolis, Kek signified darkness and was represented with the head of a frog.

KEKET: Consort of Kek at Hermopolis, she was represented as a serpent.

KHEPRI (Khepera): Associated with the rising sun, he embodied the powers of transformation and regeneration and was identified with Atum and Ra. He was represented as a scarab or as a man with a scarab face.

KHNUM (Khnemu): God of fertility and creation whose name meant "The Molder," he was often depicted as a human-headed ram fashioning men on a potter's wheel. At his temple in Elephantine he was a protector of the Nile.

KHNUMU: Nine elf-spirits who, according to the theology at Memphis, assisted Ptah in the creation. Represented as stout dwarfs with bent legs and long arms, they were placed in tombs to protect the dead.

KHONS (Chensu, Khensu): Adopted member of the Triad of Thebes, he was represented mummified with the lunar disk and crescent upon his head. He was attributed powers of exorcism and healing.

MAAT (Maa, Maot, Maati): Goddess of truth, justice, and world order, she was the representation of one of the most important abstract qualities in Egyptian theology. She was depicted as a young woman holding an ostrich feather or wearing one on her head.

MAFDET: All evildoers feared this feline goddess, who embodied the power of judicial authority. She was depicted running up a pole, which was used as a device for execution.

MESHKHENT: Goddess of maternity, she personified the bricks upon which women stood while giving birth and she prophesied the destiny of the newly born. She was represented wearing palm shoots on her head or as a brick with the head of a woman.

METHYER: Goddess associated with primeval waters, her name literally meant "the great flood." In the form of a cow she gave birth to the sky, and sometimes she was associated with Isis.

MIN (Amsu): God of fertility and vegetation, he was also sometimes worshipped as protector of travelers. His symbol was the thunderbolt and he was depicted standing, phallus erect, with one raised arm, usually holding a flail.

MNEVIS: One of the sacred bulls of Heliopolis, Mnevis was identified with the life-giving forces of the sun. In pictures of the bull, a solar disk and uraeus were placed between his horns.

MONTU: Chief deity at Hermonthis and associated with the sun and victory at war, he was later brought to Thebes and demoted to the position of Amun's adopted son. He had a falcon head surmounted by a solar disk and plumes.

MUT: Mut, her husband Amun, and their son Khons formed the Triad of Thebes. Sometimes represented wearing the headdress of a vulture, she also assumed at other times the form of a lion.

NEFERTEM: Son of Ptah and Sekhmet, he had the lotus as his symbol; he was represented as a man wearing the lotus upon his head.

NEITH: War goddess and mortuary goddess, she also taught mortals the art of weaving. At Dendera she was shown holding a tray and wearing her symbols—the bow and crossed arrows—on her head.

NEKHBET: The ancient protectress of Upper Egypt, she appeared as a woman wearing a vulture headdress surmounted by the white crown of Upper Egypt. Nekhbet and her counterpart Wadjet, the protectress of Lower Egypt, were known as "The Two Ladies" and appeared together on royal documents.

NEPHTHYS (Nebthet): Sister of Isis and Osiris and wife and sister of Seth, she was never worshipped on her own. She and Isis were so filled with grief at Osiris' death that their lamentations became known as the perfect expressions of sorrow. In the judgment scenes, she stood with Isis behind Osiris.

NUN (Nu): At Heliopolis Nun was the god of the watery chaos from which Atum arose.

NUT: Goddess of the heavens, she was believed to swallow the sun god in the evening and then give birth to him at dawn. She was often represented as a naked female bending over the earth, her hands and feet at opposite horizons.

ONURIS: Sky god often identified with Shu, he was also seen as a god of battle with the war-like qualities of Ra. In representations, he appeared as a warrior, bearded and holding a lance; on his headdress were four tall plumes.

OSIRIS: He was originally identified with the life-giving forces of water, vegetation, and soil. He was the god of the underworld and was associated with resurrection. His cult centers were at Busiris and Abydos, but he was widely worshipped. He was depicted as a mummified figure wearing the white crown with two plumes; he wore a false beard and carried the crook and flail.

PTAH: At Memphis he was the supreme god and architect of the universe. To this sublime creator was attributed the creation of all earthly forms, and even the gods were considered personifications of Ptah. In his earliest form he was seen as protector of artisans and artists. He was represented in human form, mummified, with a tight-fitting cap upon his head and a false beard; he held a scepter.

QADESH: Originally a Syrian nature goddess, she was adopted by the Egyptians as a goddess of love and beauty. She may be seen standing naked on a lion, holding lotus blossoms and papyrus. She was identified with Hathor.

QEBSENNUEF: Falcon-headed son of Horus, he was found on the canopic jar containing the intestines removed from the corpse before mummification. Associated with the western point of the compass, he and his brothers also appeared on a lotus flower before Osiris in the judgment scene.

RA (Re): Sun god of Heliopolis, Ra was the visible body of the sun. He assumed several forms: as a falcon-headed man wearing a solar disk on his head, he was known as Ra-Herakhty; as a scarab or a man with a scarab face he was the god of the morning sun, Khephri; in the Middle Kingdom, he became known as the composite god, Amun-Ra.

RA-TAIUT: "The Mistress of Heliopolis," female counterpart of Ra, she was represented in the form of a woman wearing either a disk with horns or a cobra upon her head.

RENENUTET: Goddess of fertility and the harvest who presided over the nourishment of children, she was represented as either a snake-headed female, a lion-headed female, or a woman with human attributes. She gave names, personality, and fortune to the new born.

RENPET: "The Lady of Eternity," the goddess of time, she was associated with the passage of time, youth, and the year. She was represented wearing a long palm shoot above her head.

RESHEF: Syrian god of war and battle, his name meant "lightning." He was represented bearded and carried various weapons and the ankh; on his head he wore the white crown of Upper Egypt, from which projected the horns or head of a gazelle.

SATIS: Archer goddess and wife of Khnum, she was worshipped at Elephantine and associated with the rapid currents of the Nile; her name signified "she who runs like an arrow." She wore the white crown of Upper Egypt with two antelope horns projecting from it.

SEF: One of the two protective lions guarding the passage through which the sun passed every evening. Sef ("yesterday") and his partner Dua may be later forms of the lion Aker.

SEKER: Originally a god of vegetation, he was later identified with Osiris and was worshipped at Memphis as a god of the dead, Seker-Osiris. He was represented as a hawk-headed mummy.

SEKHMET: The name of this goddess of war and battle literally meant "the powerful one." She was the consort of Ptah, and together with their son Nefertem, they made up the Triad of

Memphis. She was depicted as a woman with the head of a lioness.

SELKET: Represented wearing the scorpion on her head, she, along with Isis, Neith, and Nephthys, was protectress of coffins and canopic jars. She was also associated with the scorching heat of the Egyptian sun.

SERAPIS: This god was a composite of Osiris, the Apis bull, and various Greek deities. Serapis was a god of corn supply and of the underworld and was worshipped at the Serapeum Temple in Alexandria and Memphis.

SESHAT: To her, the wife of Thoth, was attributed the invention of letters; she was keeper of time and she helped priests establish ground plans for temples. On her head she wore a star, surmounted by a crescent moon and two plumes.

SETH (Set, Thyphon, Bebo, Smy, among others): Assassin of Osiris, Seth was an evil god associated with all that is destructive; nonetheless, he was a member of the Great Ennead and at times his energy was used as a positive force, as when he was given a place in the solar boat to protect Ra. He was depicted with a body of a man and the head of a dog-like animal.

SEVEN HATHORS: Goddesses of destiny, the Seven Hathors prophesied at birth the events to come in the life of the new-born child. In the birth houses in Graeco-Roman temples they may be seen assisting in royal births.

SHAI: This inescapable god of destiny was born with each human and lived with that person until death. At the judgment he recounted the virtues and corruptions in the life of the dead person. His female form was Shait.

SHU: He and his sister/wife were the first couple in the Great Ennead. Shu, "the uplifter," was the god of the air whose job it was to support the heavens. He was usually represented in human form with an ostrich feather on his head.

SUCHOS: Identified in some cases as an associate of Seth and as an agent of evil, he was at other times thought of as a protector of the dead. His main cult centers were in the Fayum and at Kom Ombo, and he was depicted as a crocodile or a crocodile-headed man wearing a solar disk or a uraeus.

TATJENEN: Ancient earth god of Memphis who later merged with Ptah, he was represented as a bearded man wearing a crown of two feathers, a solar disk, and rams' horns.

TAWERET: Benevolent protectress and goddess of maternity, she was especially worshipped at Thebes and was featured in the birth houses of temples. She was represented as a standing hippopotomus with a large belly.

TEFNUT: One of the Great Ennead, twin sister and wife of Shu, she was at first identified with the moon; later she became goddess of dew and rain.

THOTH (Tahuti, Tehuti): Originally a lunar deity, he became one of the most powerful and influential of the gods. He was god of wisdom and writing; he was the inventor of hieroglyphics and keeper of records for the gods. He was author of the Book of Thoth, and was closely associated with Ra. He was represented as a man with the head of either a baboon or ibis or as either of those two animals.

UNUT: Local goddess at Hermopolis, she was represented with the body of a hare holding a knife, or sometimes the scepter and ankh.

WADJET: Protectress of Lower Egypt (as Nekhbet had been protectress of Upper Egypt). Wadjet was depicted as a winged cobra, as a cobra wearing the red crown of Lower Egypt, or as a woman wearing the red crown and holding a scepter.

# Selected Bibliography

Aldred, Cyril. *Egypt to the End of the Old Kingdom.* New York: McGraw-Hill, 1965.

Anthes, Rudolf. "Mythology in Ancient Egypt" in Samuel Noah Kramer, *Mythologies of the Ancient World.* Chicago: Quadrangle Book, 1961.

Bratton, Fred Gladstone. *Myths and Legends of the Ancient Near East.* New York: Thomas Y. Crowell, 1970.

Breasted, James Henry. *Development of Religion and Thought in Ancient Egypt.* New York: Charles Scribner's Sons, 1912.

Budge, E. A. Wallis. *The Book of the Dead.* London: Routledge and Kegan Paul, 1923.

——————— *The Egyptian Heaven and Hell.* London: Martin Hopkinson, 1925.

——————— *Egyptian Religion: Egyptian Ideas for the Future Life.* London: Routledge and Kegan Paul, 1979. Reprint.

——————— *The Gods of the Egyptians, or Studies in Egyptian Mythology.* New York: Dover, 1969. Reprint.

——————— *The Nile: Notes for Travellers in Egypt.* London: Thomas Cook and Son, 1892.

——————— *Osiris and the Egyptian Resurrection.* New York: Dover, 1973. Reprint.

Campbell, Joseph. *The Flight of the Wild Gander: Explorations in the Mythological Dimension.* South Bend, In: Gateway Editions, 1969.

Cerny, Jaroslav. *Ancient Egyptian Religion.* Westport, CT: Greenwood Press, 1979.

Clark, R. T. Rundle. *Myth and Symbol in Ancient Egypt.* London: Thames and Hudson, 1959.

David, Rosalie. *Cult of the Sun: Myth and Magic in Ancient Egypt.* London: J. M. Dent and Sons, 1980.

Dennis, James Teackle. *The Burden of Isis: Being the Laments of Isis and Nephthys.* London: John Murray, 1918.

Divin, Marguerite. *Stories from Ancient Egypt.* London: Burke, 1965.

Eliade, Mircea. *Myths, Dreams, and Mysteries: The Encounter Between Contemporary Faiths and Archaic Realities.* Translated by Philip Mairet. New York: Harper and Row, 1960.

Erman, Adolf. *The Ancient Egyptians: A Sourcebook of their Writings.* Translated by Aylward M. Blackman. Gloucester, Mass.: Peter Smith, 1978.

Fairman, H. W. *The Triumph of Horus: An Ancient Egyptian Sacred Drama.* Berkeley: University of California Press, 1974.

Faulkner, R. C. *The Ancient Egyptian Coffin Texts.* Warminster, England: Aris and Phillips, 1973.

_____ *The Ancient Egyptian Pyramid Texts.* Oxford: Clarendon, 1969.

Frazer, James George. *The Golden Bough: A Study in Magic and Religion.* New York: Macmillan, 1980. Reprint.

Frye, Northrop. *The Great Code: The Bible and Literature.* New York: Harcourt Brace Jovanovich, 1982.

Goodrich, Norma Lorre. *Ancient Myths.* New York: The New American Library, 1960.

Grayson, A. Kirk and Donald B. Redford. *Papyrus and Tablet.* Englewood Cliffs, N.J.: Prentice-Hall, 1973.

Griffins, J. Gwyn. *The Conflict of Horus and Seth from Egyptian and Classical Sources: A Study in Ancient Mythology.* Liverpool: Liverpool University Press, 1960.

Grimal, Pierre. *Larousse World Mythology.* New York: G. P. Putnam's Sons, 1965.

*A Guide to the Egyptian Museum.* Cairo: General Egyptian Book Organization, 1980.

*Guidebook to the Luxor Museum of Ancient Egyptian Art.* Cairo: Egyptian Antiquities Organization, 1978.

Herodotus. *The Histories.* Translated by Aubrey de Selincourt. New York: Penguin, 1972.

Hook, S. H. *Middle Eastern Mythology.* Baltimore: Penguin, 1963.

_____ *Myth, Ritual and Kingship: Essays on the Theory and Practice of Kingship in the Ancient Near East and in Israel.* Oxford: Clarendon, 1958.

Hurry, Jamison B. *Imhotep: The Vizar and Physician of King Zozer and Afterwards the Egyptian God of Medicine.* Chicago: Ares, 1978.

James, E. C. *The Cult of the Mother-Goddess: An Archaeological and Documentary Study.* New York: Barnes and Noble, 1959.

──────── *Myth and Ritual in the Ancient Near East.* New York: Frederick A. Praegar, 1958.

Kamil, Jill. *Luxor: A guide to Ancient Thebes.* London: Longman, 1976.

──────── *Sakkara: A Guide to the Necropolis of Sakkara and the Site of Memphis.* London: Longman, 1978.

Kees, Hermann. *Ancient Egypt: A Cultural Topography.* Translateed by Ian F. D. Morrow. Chicago: The University of Chicago Press, 1961.

James, T. G. H. *Myths and Legends of Ancient Egypt.* New York: Grosset and Dunlap, 1971.

Lichtheim, Miriam. *Ancient Egyptian Literature: A Book of Readings.* Berkeley: University of California Press, 1973.

Lurker, Manfred. *The Gods and Symbols of Ancient Egypt: An Illustrated Dictionary.* Translated by Barbara Cummings. London: Thames and Hudson, 1980.

MacQuitty, William. *Island of Isis: Philae, Temple of the Nile.* London: Macdonald and Janes, 1976.

Mercatante, Anthony S. *Who's Who in Egyptian Mythology.* New York: Clarkson N. Potter, 1978.

Meyerowitz, Eva L. R. *The Divine Kingship in Ghana and Ancient Egypt.* London: Faber and Faber, 1960.

Morenz, Siegfried. *Egyptian Religion.* Translated by Ann E. Keep. Ithaca, NY: Cornell University Press, 1973.

Murray, M. A. *Ancient Egytian Legends.* London: John Murray, 1920.

Murray, Margaret A. *The Splendour That Was Egypt.* London: Sidgwick and Jackson, 1963.

Patrick, Richard. *All Color Book of Egyptian Mythology.* London: Octopus Books, 1972.

Petrie, W. M. Flinders. *Egyptian Tales: Translated from the Papyri.* New York: Benjamin Bloom, 1971.

──────── *The Religion of Ancient Egypt.* London: Archibald Constable, 1906.

──────── *Religious Life in Ancient Egypt.* Boston: Houghton Mifflin, 1924.

Piankoff, Alexandre. *Mythological Papyri.* New York: Pantheon Books, 1957.

Plutarch. "Isis and Osiris" in *Plutarch's Moralia.* Translated by Frank Cole Babbitt. Cambridge, MA: Harvard University Press, 1962.

Prichard, James B. *The Ancient Near East: An Anthology of Texts and Pictures.* Princeton, NJ: Princeton University Press, 1958.

Rossiter, Evelyn. *The Book of the Dead: Papyri of Ani, Hunefer, Anhai.* Fribourg-Geneve: Productions Liber SA and Editions Minerva SA, 1979.

Sauneron, Serge. *The Priests of Ancient Egypt.* Translated by Ann Morrissett. New York: Grove Press, 1969.

Shorter, Alan W. *The Egyptian Gods: A Handbook.* London: Routledge and Kegan Paul, 1937. Reprint.

Simpson, William Kelly, ed. *The Literature of Ancient Egypt. An Anthology of Stories, Instructions, and Poetry.* New Haven: Yale University Press, 1972.

Steindorff, George and Keith C. Seele. *When Egypt Ruled the East.* Chicago: Chicago University Press, 1957.

Velde, H. T. *Seth, God of Confusion: A Study of His Role in Egyptian Mythology and Religion.* London: Leiden, 1967.

Witt, R. E. *Isis in the Graeco-Roman World.* Ithaca, NY: Cornell University Press, 1971.

# Index

*References to plates are printed in bold-face type.*

Aahmes, 141, 144
Abtu, 60
Abu Gurob, 16
Abu Simbel, 30, 89, 97, 119, 136, 159, 167, 178
Abydos, 41, 42, 45, 50, 57, 76, 83, 118, 136, 177, 195
Achilles, 102
Adonis, 86
Agricultural Museum, Cairo, 136
Ahura, 158
Aker, 190, 192, 196
Aldred, Cyril, 16
Alexander the Great, 12
Alexandria, 197
Amaunet, 138, 154, 190
Amen, 114
Amenhetep III, 130, 148
Amenhetep IV, **42**, 14, 191
Amenophis II, 118
Ammit, **49**, 170, 190
Amun, 28, 137-151, 154, 167, 190, 194
Amun-Ra, **40**, 28, 136, 138, 141-144, 186, 190, 196
Amun-Ra-Khamutef. *See* Min
Anedjti, 42, 190
Ankh, 24, 26, 48, 80, 124, 130, 132, 144, 148, 160, 182, 190, 191, 193, 196, 198
Annu, 15, 16, 32, 113, 153, 156
Ant, 60
Anthat, 191
Anthes, Rudolf, 86
Anty, 104, 106
Anubis, **48, 50,** 12, 28, 36, 44, 54, 57, 75, 78, 82, 83, 86, 95, 144, 168-177, 191
Anuket, 184
Anukis, 191
Apes, 66, 159, 192
Apis, **35,** 122, 123, 136, 191, 197
Apohis, 138
Apophis, 30, 52, 60, 61, 138, 191

Arabia, 73
Artemis, 50
Aso, 74
Astarte, 191
Asti, 66
Aswan, 44, 48, 102, 113, 118, 132, 177, 178, 182, 191
Atef crown, 42
Aten, **42,** 153, 191
Athenais, 75, 76
Attis, 86
Atum, **7,** 26, 30, 60, 69, 71, 92, 123, 153, 154, 155, 191, 193, 195
Atum-Ra, **40,** 103, 104, 106, 108, 109
Baboons, **46,** 30, 97, 160, 198
Bael, 191
Bast, 127
Bastet, 130, 191
Bata, 172-177
Beer, 16, 44, 73, 113, 116, 159, 174
Bekhten, 150-151
Benben stone, 16
Bennu, 61
Bes, **143,** 12, 144, 191
Bible, the, 191
Blood of Isis, **15,** 48
Book of Breathings, 156
Book of Dead, 11, 24, 28, 31, **34,** 41, 45, 48, 56, 61, 62, 85, 95, 116, 126, 130, 132, 148, 156, 160, 164, 167, 170, 177, 182
Book of the Gates, 93
Book of Thoth, 126-128, 156-159, 198
Breasted, James, 75
British Museum, London, 41, 70
Bubastis, 127, 191
Buchis, 192
Budge, E.A. Wallis, 31, 48, 70, 86, 162, 164
Burisis, 42, 85, 190, 195
Byblos, 46, 75, 76
Cairo, 15, 28, 97, 118, 120, 136, 178
Calendar, 22
Campbell, Joseph, 188
Canopic jars, 56, 192, 193, 196, 197

Cats, 30, 61, 130, 191
Chemmis, 74
Cheops, 64-65
Christ. See Jesus
Cippi of Horus, 89
Clark, R.T. Rundle, 85, 88, 92
Cobras, 20, 22, 30, 34, 68, 128, 130, 182,
    194, 196, 197, 198
Coffin Texts, 30, 31, 34, 41, 45, 61, 92,
    95, 110, 114, 156, 164, 168, 181
Coomaraswamy, Ananda K., 189
Cows, 40, 65, 114, 117, 118, 173, 192, 193
Creation. See Myths
Crocodiles. See Myths, 82, 92, 99, 117,
    141, 150, 170, 190, 197
David, Rosalie, 62
Dedi, 64
Deir el Bahari, 118, 141
Delta, the, 45, 54, 75, 78, 85, 92, 148, 153
Dendera, 32, 36, 40, 45, 78, 114, 117, 118,
    192, 195
Diana, 50
Diodorus, 82, 84
Djed pillar, 77, 45, 48, 76, 84-86, 124
Djehuty, 140
Dogs, 168
Dua, 192, 196
Duamutef, 192
Earth Mother, 110, 116, 119
Edfu, 32, 54, 92, 97, 117, 193
Egyptian Museum, Cairo, 38, 41, 50, 54,
    56, 97, 118, 136, 159, 160, 167, 177
El Ashuein, 159
Elephantine Island, 14, 113, 182, 184, 192,
    193, 196
Ethiopia, 73, 74
Eye, the, 28, 20, 32, 34, 69, 70, 83, 93,
    102, 113, 119, 130, 138, 156
Falcons, 27, 30, 89, 92, 97, 192, 194, 196
Falsehood, 165-167
Fayum, 192, 197
Feast of Khoiak, 45
Festival of Behdet, 117
Feather, 160, 162, 164, 190, 191, 194, 198
First Fruits, 117
Fish, 83, 159, 173
Frazer, James, 22, 86
Frogs, 192, 193
Frye, Northrop, 12
Gazelles, 196

Geb, 10, 18, 22, 31, 36-38, 40, 41, 66, 89,
    112, 182, 192
Gebel Silsileh, 192
Geese, 34
Genesis, 15
Gerbner, George, 189
Goats, 117
Great Ennead, 18, 22, 36, 41, 50, 56, 58,
    123, 124, 174, 192, 197, 198
Greece, 50
Hapi, 51, 24, 60, 178-182, 192
Hapy, 192
Harpocrates, 26, 89
Hather, 33, 34, 31, 40, 48, 65, 89, 92, 102,
    104, 110-118, 130, 144, 187, 191,
    192, 193, 196
Hatshepsut, 118, 141-144, 192
Hawks, 23, 28, 97, 117, 148, 151, 196
Hector, 102
Heget, 142, 144
Heh, 154, 192
Heket, 64, 154, 192
Heliopolis, 14, 15, 16, 18, 28, 36, 44, 61,
    62, 64, 89, 92, 95, 103, 122, 123, 154,
    191, 192, 193, 194, 195, 196
Herakhty, 28, 192
Hermonthis, 192, 194
Hermopolis, 128, 153-154, 160, 193, 198
Herodotus, 53, 61, 140
Hershef, 193
Hikapath, 120
Hippopotamuses, 102, 103, 106, 117, 138,
    170, 190, 198
Horus, 25, 30, 12, 18, 22, 28, 36, 42, 44,
    45, 46, 48, 49, 52, 54, 60, 61, 69, 70,
    71, 78, 80, 82, 83, 84, 86, 89, 92, 97, 98,
    99-109, 116, 117, 118, 123, 142, 144,
    155, 164, 170, 186, 192, 193, 196
Iat, 144
Ibis, 66, 134, 159, 160, 198
Ihy, 110, 193
Ikhnaton. See Amenhetep IV
Illiad, The, 98
Imhotep, 39, 132-135, 136, 193
Imsety, 93
Isaaset, 193
Isis, 14, 22, 23, 12, 18, 22, 36, 42, 44, 45-
    50, 52, 55, 56, 57, 60, 64, 65, 66-71, 72-
    88, 89, 92, 95, 102, 103, 104, 106, 108,
    110, 114, 119, 124, 155, 168, 170, 187,

193, 194, 195, 197
Iusaset, 31
Jackels, 54, 168, 170, 191, 192
Jaffa. *See* Joppa
Jesus, 132, 182
Joppa, 138, 140
Joseph, father of Jesus, 15
Judgment of souls. *See* Myths: trial of the
  souls
Karnak, 28, 130, 136, 142, 146, 148
Kek, 154, 193
Keket, 154, 193
Khepri, **6**, 26, 28, 30, 60, 69, 117, 154,
  155, 193, 196
Khnum, **52**, 50, 64, 132, 142, 144, 174,
  180, 182, 191, 193, 196
Khnumu, 194
Khons, **44**, 137, 140, 148-151, 194
Khons Neferhetep. *See* Khons
Kom Ombo, 54, 150, 193, 197
Koptos, 74, 137, 158, 184
Lake Nasser, 32
Lion, 128, 130, 132, 170, 190, 192, 194,
  195, 197
Lotus, **13**, 11, 42, 130, 132, 192, 193, 194,
  196
Lower Egypt, 11, 34, 36, 42, 78, 120, 123,
  138, 148, 181, 191, 192, 195, 198
Lucifer, 52
Lunar disk, 160
Lurker, Manfred, 57, 85
Luxor, 28, 40, 50, 57, 60, 97, 118, 136,
  137, 146, 182, 186
Maat, **47**, 24, 42, 124, 148, 152-167, 188,
  194
*Maat,* as a concept, 162-164
Mafdet, 194
Magic, 48, 61
Malkander, 75
Manetho, 15
Mary, mother of Jesus, 16, 48
Matet, 60
Medicine, 48, 134
Medinet Habu, 186
Memphis, 14, 16, 84, 120, 136, 137, 148,
  152, 191, 194, 195, 197
Memphite theology, 122-124
Menat necklace, 116, 124
Meskhent, 64, 144, 194

Methyer, 194
Meyerowitz, Eva R., 187
Min, **53**, 137, 184, 187, 194
Minia, 146, 153, 159, 160
Mnevis, 194
Montu, 137, 194
Moon, 20, 22, 34, 53, 66, 93, 117, 123,
  148, 150, 155, 187, 191
Morenz, Siegfried, 16, 88, 89, 93, 154, 162
Murray, M.A., 70
Mut, **43**, 130, 136, 137, 146-148, 194
Myths
  Amun-Ra as divine parent, 141-144;
  blinding of Truth, 164-167;
  concepts of, 12;
  creation, 12, 18, 26, 31, 58, 110, 122,
  123, 124, 164, 182, 184, 194;
  creation at Hermopolis, 153-154;
  creation of the black race, 93;
  creation of the sun and moon, 32;
  daily voyage of Ra through the sky, **18,**
  58-61;
  destruction of mankind, 28, 112-114;
  festival of Min, **53**, 186-187;
  Horus' battle with Seth, **30**, 98-109;
  judgment of souls. *See* Myths: trial of
  souls
  Khnum and potter's wheel, **52**, 182;
  Khnum and the drought, 182, 184;
  murder of Osiris and Isis' hunt for his
  body, **22**, 72-88;
  Nut and her children, **11**, 40;
  Power of Khons, **44**, 150-151;
  Ptah as royal protector, **36**, 126-128;
  Ra as royal father, **4**, 62-65;
  Ra in his declining years, 65-66;
  Ra kisses Maat, 164;
  secret name of Ra, 66-71;
  sun god and the phoenix, **19**, 61-62;
  tale of the two brothers, 172-177;
  Tefnut and her anger, **9**, 32;
  trial of souls, **2**, 34, 44, 48, 95, 164,
  167, 193, 195, 196;
Naunet, 154
Nectanebo I, 50
Neferkapath, 126-128, 158-159
Nefertem, **38**, 123, 130-132, 194, 196
Nefertari, 119
Nehebka, 60

Neith, **31, 56,** 103, 197
Nekhbet, 195, 198
Nephthys, **17,** 18, 22, 36, 44, 48, 54-57, 64, 75, 78, 82, 83, 124, 168, 195, 197
Nile, 24, 31, 42, 48, 53, 56, 74, 82, 113, 120, 137, 153, 158, 160, 178, 180, 181, 182, 183, 184, 192, 193, 196
Nubia, 32, 99
Nun, **3,** 20, 30, 40, 58, 60, 65, 112, 114, 138, 154, 164, 181, 195
Nut, **11, 12, 20,** 18, 20, 22, 31, 34, 36-41, 53, 56, 65-66, 89, 110, 112, 192, 195
On. See Annu and Heliopolis
Onuris, 195
Opening of the Mouth, 83, 95, 117, 126, 170
Osiris, **5, 13, 22, 23, 24, 43, 79, 87,** 18, 22, 30, 34, 36, 41-45, 47, 48, 52, 54, 56, 57, 72-88, 89, 92, 93, 95, 102, 103, 104, 108, 117, 124, 130, 155, 164, 168-170, 178, 182, 190, 192, 193, 195, 196, 197
Oxen, 117
Palestine, 50
Pamyles, 73
Panopolis, 184
Papremis, 53
Papyrus of Anhai, 30
Papyrus of Ani, 28, 34
Papyrus of Hunefer, 30, 34
Papyrus of Nisti-Ta-Nebet-Taui, 170
Pe, 78, 82
Peger, 84
Petosiris, 160
Petrie, Flinders, 123, 168
Philae, 45, 48, 84, 114, 118, 134, 135
Phoenix, **19,** 30, 61-62
Piankhi, 15
Plato, 15, 189
Pig, 102
Plutarch, 22, 45, 50, 53, 72, 83, 170, 189
Primeval waters, 20
Ptah, **36,** 85, 108, 123-136, 145, 153, 180, 186, 193, 195, 196, 197
Ptolemy II, 15, 50, 97
Ptolemy V, 135
Pyramid of Unas, 40, 130
Pyramids of Giza, 65
Pyramid Texts, 20, 36, 38, 40, 41, 45, 52, 56, 72, 85, 123, 153, 154, 156, 181, 182

Pythagoras, 15
Qadseh, 185
Qebsennuef, 196
Ra, **4, 18,** 11, 15, 16, 18, 20, 22, 24, 26, 30, 31-41, 46, 52, 53, 58-71, 82, 89, 93, 99, 110-114, 130-132, 137, 153-155, 164, 168-170, 180, 181, 191, 192, 193, 195, 196, 197
Ra-Herakhty, 28, 89, 92, 99, 173, 174, 196
Ram, 140, 182, 192, 198
Ramesses II, 28, 45, 53, 54, 97, 118, 119, 122-128, 135, 136, 159
Ramesses III, 54, 57, 141, 151, 186
Ramesses VI, 40
Red-dedet, 64
Renenutet, 196
Renpet, 196
Reshef, 196
Rome, 50
Sacred marriage, the. See Myths
Sakkara, 12, 40, 50, 85, 122, 126, 130, 132, 134, 191, 193
Sako, 172
Satis, 184, 191, 196
Scepter, 22, 26, 42, 92, 124, 148, 160, 182, 190, 198
Scorpions, 158, 197
Scarab, 26, 30, 193, 196
Sebau, 60
Sef, 192, 196
Seker, 196
Seker-Osiris. See Seker
Sekhmet, **37,** 93, 110, 113, 123, 128-130, 132, 148, 194, 196
Seknenre, 138
Selket, 56, 197
Semket, 60
Senet, 126
Serapis, 197
Serpents, 60, 66, 191, 193
Seshat, 197
Sesostris I, 16
Seth, **16, 30, 32,** 18, 22, 34, 36, 41, 44, 48, 50-54, 56, 57, 73-75, 78-83, 84, 86, 89, 92, 93, 98-109, 117, 123, 124, 155, 156, 168, 191, 195, 197
Seti I, 28, 45, 50, 53, 54, 57, 66, 86, 118, 136, 160
Setna, 126-128

Setna Khaemuast, 126
Seven Hathors, 174, 197
Shai, 197
Shait, 197
Shepenkhonsu, 57
Shu, **8, 12,** 18, 20, 30-31, 34, 38, 40, 65,
    103, 112, 182, 184, 195, 197, 198
Sistrum, 116, 193
Snakes, 61, 158, 196
Sokaris, 124
Solar boat, **18,** 16, 26, 30, 38, 40, 41, 52,
    58, 80-82, 83, 92, 93, 109, 110, 152,
    155, 164, 197
Solar disk, **29,** 22, 28, 30, 34, 48, 56, 89,
    92, 99, 102, 112, 114, 128, 191
Solon, 15
Step Pyramid, 85, 132, 193
Suchos, 197
Sun, 20, 26, 32, 34, 40, 52, 53, 58, 61, 62,
    66, 69, 93, 116, 123, 128, 130, 146,
    154, 155, 182, 192, 196, 197
Syria, 75
Ta Tenen, 123
Tabubu, 127
Tatjenen, 197
Taweret, 198
Tefen, 80
Tefnut, **33,** 18, 20, 30, 31, 32, 34, 38, 112,
    198
Tel el Armarna, 146
Thales, 15
Thebes, 14, 28, 73, 74, 124, 134, 137, 151,

152, 190, 194, 198
Thenen, 135
Thoth, **45, 46,** 12, 22, 24, 32, 36, 44, 48,
    53, 60, 64, 66, 72, 73, 78, 82, 83, 93,
    95, 97, 99, 103, 104, 108, 126, 134, 135,
    142, 144, 148, 152-167, 189, 197, 198
Thothmes III, 54, 136, 140
Thutmose I, 141
Tounah el Gebel, 160
Trial of souls. *See* Myths
Truth (*Maat*), **47,** 164-167
Tuat, 60, 68
Turin, 70
Tutankamun, 50, 56, 57, 118, 132, 136,
    146, 160, 177
Uazet, 78
Unut, 198
Upper Egypt, 11, 24, 36, 42, 45, 50, 74,
    120, 137, 138, 141, 148, 160, 181,
    182, 191, 195, 196, 198
Uraeus. *See* Cobras
Userkaf, 65
Valley of Cedars, 176, 178
Valley of the Kings, 28, 50, 54, 160, 167
Valley of the Tuat, 26
Vulture, 48, 148, 150, 193, 194, 195
Wadjet, 195, 198
Wast, 137
Waset, 137
Wine, 73, 74, 116
Winged disk. *See* solar disk
Zozer, 132, 182, 193

Produced by the Printshop
of
the American University in Cairo Press